Praise for *This Is China*

It is hard to imagine that such a short book can cover such a vast span of time and space. This Is China: The First 5,000 Years *will help teachers, students, and general readers alike, as they seek for a preliminary guide to the contexts and complexities of Chinese culture.*

Jonathan Spence, professor of history, Yale University; author of *The Search for Modern China*

In this slim volume, tiny by comparison with its regiments of oversize competitors in the crowded field of general histories of China, a team of experts has performed the miracle of distilling their collective knowledge into a seamless and lucid essay on Chinese geography, prehistory, history, and culture. One must marvel at the skill with which the editors have reconciled and synthesized the wide range of contributors' ideas and opinions and combined them into such a coherent, convincing, elegant, and engaging whole. The study draws its material from the five volumes of the Berkshire Encyclopedia of China, *launched last year to critical acclaim and now on its way toward becoming a major reference book on Chinese history, society, and thought. Students will enjoy the sparse but richly supported narrative. Teachers everywhere will welcome it as a classroom aid and a virtuoso contribution to the genre of short books on China.*

Gregor Denton, professor of Chinese history, Cardiff University

I only wish I had had This Is China: The First 5,000 Years *available during my fifteen years of teaching Chinese at the college level. It provides a superb historically based foundation for the beginning language student to understand the importance of those "first 5,000 years" in shaping the modern language. The inclusion of the Chinese characters and pinyin for each of the section headings is an added bonus. Together with web-based supplementary material made available by the publisher,* This Is China *is a tremendous resource for both Chinese language students and teachers, and I recommend it highly.*

Scott McGinnis, academic advisor and professor, Defense Language Institute, Washington DC

This is a gem. It is a reference that everyone who teaches, writes, or thinks about China should have close at hand. Each section is concise, literate, and well written. The information presented is very up-to-date, including descriptions of China's scientific accomplishments, the contributions of women to the development of Chinese culture, the ways in which China has always been linked by trade and by intellectual interaction to the global development of human civilization, and how new archaeological discoveries are changing the ways we define China's past. This stimulating and rewarding approach is carried through to discussions of the economic, intellectual, and values debates our colleagues in China are currently engaged in. At a time when Chinese is rapidly becoming the most important second-language for millions worldwide, the inclusion of Chinese characters at many points in the text

(continued)

is both welcome and necessary. What's more, the characters are accompanied by pinyin transliteration with tone marks, meaning that even beginning students will rapidly increase their ability to read and speak Chinese. Don't be caught without this book.

Ronald Suleski, professor and director, Rosenberg
Institute for East Asian Studies, Suffolk University

China today is an economic superpower, competing in every arena of human endeavor. From trade, business and finance to diplomacy, defense and security; from science, technology and innovation to culture, media and sports—China's growing strengths have global implications. Foreigners need to understand the deep history of China, because in China the past profoundly affects the present. It is hard to imagine a more accessible, accurate book than This Is China: The First 5,000 Years.

Robert Lawrence Kuhn, international investment
banker, corporate strategist; author of *How China's
Leaders Think*

Ambitious, sweeping, and of necessity efficiently economical and compressed, This Is China: The First 5,000 Years *packs about as much of the panorama of the Chinese experience into a single volume as is physically possible. For those of us who still enjoy the pleasures of physical reference books, this one is a must, as it is for the expanding universe of those who know that understanding China will be increasingly important in their lives.*

Dan Burstein, managing partner, Millennium
Technology Ventures; author of *Big Dragon*

This little book should quickly become the first port of call for teachers seeking information on the vast range of topics and issues that arise while teaching a language and culture more than 5,000 years in existence. It is authoritative, easily accessed and directs the seeker to deeper information if required. It is a reference book which fills the gap constantly experienced by teachers of Chinese between too much information on some topics and nothing at all on many others of interest to their students.

Jane Orton, director, Australian Chinese Teacher
Training Centre, University of Melbourne

It is a remarkable achievement to tell China's millennia of recorded history and analyze the country's rich culture and current events in a beautifully illustrated book of 130 pages. The narrative is lucid, engaging, and insightful. This Is China: The First 5,000 Years *is a much-needed handbook for anyone who is interested in acquainting themselves with China and the Chinese in a few hours of reading.*

Hanchao Lu, Georgia Institute of Technology

This Is China

The First 5,000 Years

This Is China

The First 5,000 Years

Haiwang Yuan 袁海旺

General Editor

Ronald G. Knapp, Margot E. Landman, and Gregory Veeck

Editors

BERKSHIRE PUBLISHING GROUP

Great Barrington, Massachusetts

Published by:
Berkshire Publishing Group LLC
120-122 Castle Street
Great Barrington, Massachusetts 01230
www.berkshirepublishing.com
宝库山 互联世界参照点

Berkshire Publishing specializes in international relations, cross-cultural communications, global business and economic information, and environmental sustainability.

This Is China, along with *This Fleeting World*, is part of Berkshire's "This World of Ours" series. Further books in the series include *This Is Islam* and *This Good Earth*.

Illustration credits: Cover photo by Wang Ying. Interior photos come from the U.S. Library of Congress and from Joan Lebold Cohen, whose photos illustrate the *Berkshire Encyclopedia of China*.

Printed in the United States of America

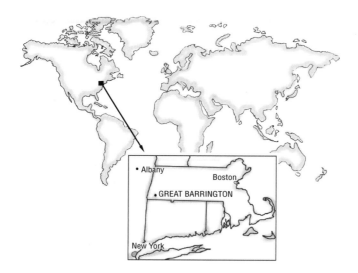

Library of Congress Cataloging-in-Publication Data
Yuan, Haiwang.
    This is China : the first 5,000 years / Haiwang Yuan.—1st ed.
        p. cm.—(This world of ours ; 2)
    Includes bibliographical references and index.
    ISBN 978-1-933782-20-1 -- ISBN 978-1-933782-76-8 (ELECTRONIC)
    1. China—History.   2. China—Civilization.   I. Title.
    DS735.Y78 2010
    951—dc22   2010007974

Editorial Board

Publisher's Note 出版人寄语

This Is China—probably the shortest survey of Chinese history, geography, and culture that exists—was made possible by a much longer work, the 2,754-page *Berkshire Encyclopedia of China: Modern and Historic Views of the World's Newest and Oldest Global Power*. In Chinese terms, even that is a short work: the *Yongle dadian*, or *Great Compendium of the Yongle Reign* (1408) had 22,877 chapters in 11,095 volumes. It was our longer encyclopedic work that made this brief history possible.

Chinese people, of course, understand the importance of brevity. And their society, as readers new to Chinese history will learn, has been one of many "firsts." The *Laozi* 老子, one of China's most renowned philosophical works, famously declared that a journey of a thousand miles begins with a single step. *This Is China*, for those of us who are learning about the country, provides an easy way to take that first, single step through thousands of years of history and across the vast territory that is China today.

This history opens a window on contemporary China—with balanced, nonpolitical coverage—by providing our readers with details about Chinese governance, society, and culture through the ages. Even our cover design reflects the modern and the ancient. By choosing a scene cropped from a 2008 photograph of the Wuyang River in Zhenyuan, Guizhou Province, where a fisherman casts his line into the water, we evoke images depicted in thousands of traditional Chinese paintings. The cover also shows lines from a sacred Buddhist scroll called the Diamond Sutra. A copy dated 868 CE was discovered in western China's Dunhuang caves in 1907, which makes it the oldest extant printed book (and a natural fascination for a publisher). The caves, located in an oasis along the old Silk Roads, are among the most magical of sites to visit in China today. Both Zhenyuan and Dunhuang remind us that historic China lives on.

The Chinese title of this book is not an exact translation of the English, but instead is based on the advice of LE La (乐拉), a young Beijing-based friend. When we explained the concept of the book to her one summer morning in Easthampton, New York, she suggested we take a more colloquial approach—"Look! This is China" (瞧！这是中国). For our readers who are studying the Chinese language we include pinyin transliterations and characters for many Chinese words and terms. Perhaps even general readers will make use of Chinese words with nuanced meanings that are impossible to translate in a single English word—like *guanxi*, a fluctuating network of relationships.

We hope that our Chinese friends will enjoy how we have presented their country to the world. We urge them, as well as all our readers, to share the book, to discuss the "thought experiments," and to send us corrections and ideas for future editions and for other China-focused publications.

《这就是中国：头一个五千年》也许是美国目前概述中国历史、地理和文化篇幅最小的书籍，其背后却以2754页的《宝库山中华全书：跨越历史和现代审视最新和最古老的全球大国》作为依托。当然，《宝库山中华全书》与11095卷，22877册的《永乐大典》这部鸿篇巨制相比，不可同日而语。

但是中国人深知言简意赅的好处，也深谙老子"千里之行，始于足下"的重要意义。对于我们这些有志于了解中国的西方人来说，这本小书在纵横幅员辽阔的中国来审视其几千年历史的征途中，只是跬步而已。

《这就是中国：头一个五千年》这一书名并非英文的确切翻译。英语原文比较口语化，是北京一位叫乐拉的年轻朋友建议的："瞧！这是中国"。我们有意为西方读者打开一扇了解今日中国的窗户。书的封面是中国一个小镇的渔民正在撒网捕鱼。此情此景见于万卷中国国画，如此设计旨在把古老和现代的中国串联起来。

希望中国的朋友们能够欣赏我们为把他们的祖国介绍给全世界所作出的努力。我们呼吁中国朋友和读者把这本书推介给更多的人，并充分讨论书中"思想实验室"中提出的问题。书中如有谬误，敬请转告，也请及时把新的想法反馈给我们，这对我们今后再版该书或出版其他关注中国的书籍是十分有益的。

Karen Christensen 沈凯伦

Founder and CEO, Berkshire Publishing Group 宝库山, Great Barrington, Massachusetts

Contents

这 就 是 中 国

CHAPTER THREE

A Century of Change—From 1912 to Today 73

CHAPTER FOUR

China Today 111

RESOURCES 127

INDEX 129

Introduction

*D*uring President Barack Obama's first visit to China in November 2009, he addressed a group of Shanghai students and proclaimed that no big issues in the world today could be resolved without cooperation between the United States and China. His trip coincided with the debut of *2012*, a disaster film in which world leaders band together in the midst of impending calamity. The movie, which makes China the manufacturer of the gigantic arks that salvage the last of the humanity from global cataclysm, served as a fitting footnote to the president's speech.

Major changes have been taking place in China since it opened to the world and began epoch-making economic reforms in the late 1970s. The president's speech and the movie both envisage, in different ways, what might lie ahead, and what role China might need to play in our common future.

Indeed, China is poised to be the world's second largest economy, with its gross domestic product (GDP) having increased to 4.91 trillion U.S. dollars in 2009 from 53 billion U.S. dollars in 1978. As 2010 begins, China is the world's largest Internet user and has the world's largest mobile phone network. It has built a total of 50,000 kilometers (31,250 miles) of superhighway (second only to the United States) since 1988, when it had none at all. It boasts the world's first commercial maglev system (magnetic levitation system, used to guide and propel vehicles) and the fastest high-speed train system with trains that run from 200 to 350 kilometers (124 to 218 miles) per hour.

At the same time, China continues to face enormous challenges: a huge population in a developing country with limited natural resources; an uneven regional development; a gap between rich and poor as great as anywhere in the world (a disparity that could lead to social and political unrest); disputes over territory; and ethnic and religious tensions. Many people debate whether a nation with a one-party government system can effectively address such domestic issues (never mind international ones).

On one side are those who believe that a two-or-more-party system is essential to success and stability in the twenty-first century. Others, in China and the West, argue that China's system, though in need of reform, is actually the most effective way to manage a huge territory and meet the needs of a huge population. Can China fix what needs fixing within its current system/structure and become a constructive force to help build a better future for the world? *This Is China* does not attempt to provide that answer, but instead gives the big picture in a short space, providing background you can use to judge China-related events as they develop.

Understanding China depends on knowing China better. There's long been an idea in the West that China and the Chinese are inscrutable—that is, hard to understand. Significant differences can make communication a problem, but we are all human, and we face the same challenges and have the same basic needs. China has its own rich history and long-established values and customs, and when Westerners get confused it's usually because they unwittingly make assumptions and judgments based on their own cultures. Karen Christensen, the publisher of *This Is China*, says that when she and her family first began traveling in China, and would comment on an aspect of Chinese life or government policy that seemed puzzling or surprising, they repeatedly heard the phrase, "Well, this is China," and "But this is China." That became the inspiration for the title of our book.

By choosing the subtitle, *The First 5,000 Years*, we intended to be amusing, to make you wonder about the "next 5,000 years." Such telescoping vision comes naturally to fans of science fiction who love to imagine the future, although perhaps not as it plays out in *2012. This Is China* focuses on the distant and more recent past, but it is intended to equip students, teachers, and professionals to face the challenges of the present and the great questions that lie ahead. We realize that some scholars think "five thousand years" exaggerates the length of Chinese civilization. Please read the book to see where the different measures come from—and what different people mean by civilization, too.

This Is China includes four major sections. Chapter 1 provides background about China's physical and human geographies. Chapter 2 offers an overview of China from prehistory to the end of the last dynasty in 1911/12. Chapter 3 introduces a century of change since 1912. Finally, chapter 4 deals with cultural concepts and ideas that have shaped the way Chinese in the twenty-first century interact with themselves and others. Just as importantly, it addresses concerns and challenges the Chinese and their leaders face today.

With information on every aspect of China selected from the five-volume *Berkshire Encyclopedia of China* and other sources, and checked by experts inside and outside China, *This Is China* makes every effort to provide authentic, accurate, and timely information about China's history—as much as that is possible when dealing with a complex, continuous culture over millennia—and to do so without a political agenda. Nonetheless, we encourage you to approach the book, as you do any other, with critical thinking and an open mind.

This concise 120-page volume is designed to be read straight through, as a short, eye-opening course in contemporary and historic China, or to be dipped into for facts and intriguing sidebars, as well as maps and illustrations. It can be used in curriculum development and as an adjunct to courses—in social studies, international relations, international business, world history, political science, or Chinese language. (We include Chinese characters, as well as pinyin transliterations, since many young people and adults are learning Chinese and because communication—becoming familiar and comfortable with different forms of expressing ideas and information—is the foundation of human culture.)

To supplement and enhance classroom use of the book, we will make two Web-based resources available free of charge: a questionnaire and a selection of Chinese proverbs related to the book's specific contents. We'll also provide links to the *Berkshire Encyclopedia of China* and other online sites that address the following topics:

- Migration and urbanization
- Foreign relations—and not just with the United States
- Religion
- Regional conflicts
- Ethnicity
- Political development
- Women's rights and roles in China
- Press freedom and censorship
- And much, much more

Finally, we provide a list of sources (including books, articles, and movies) and organizations we consider most valuable—and balanced—and urge readers to send us their own discoveries as they continue to learn about China.

Many people have been involved in making this book possible. Besides the contributors to the articles we have selected, I'm particularly grateful to Karen and Rachel Christensen, along with their Berkshire Publishing team, for helping me assemble this material. Berkshire's senior editor, Mary Bagg, has not only edited the text, but she has excerpted and harmonized the work of a highly varied group of contributing authors, and added many grace notes, too.

It does take a special effort—and the right teachers—to reach a point of understanding and familiarity with China. As a Chinese saying goes: "A master only leads one into the gate of a temple; it's up to that individual to learn to be a real monk (师父领进门, 修行靠个人 Shīfu lǐng jìn mén,xiūxíng kào gèrén)." If this book can show its readers to China's door and arouse their interest in learning more about the country—the land and the people—then it will serve its purpose.

I sincerely hope that *This Is China* will make a contribution to the understanding of Chinese history, culture, and current events. Facing common global challenges, we need a sense of common purpose based on understanding and respect, so we can share this planet—our ark—and live harmoniously together.

Haiwang Yuan
Western Kentucky University Libraries

About the Editor

Haiwang Yuan, now a U.S. citizen, came from China in 1988 as a Fulbright student and graduated from Indiana University at Bloomington with degrees in history and library science.

Yuan served as an associate editor of the *Berkshire Encyclopedia of China* (2009); he was a contributor to the *Encyclopedia of Contemporary Chinese Culture* (Routledge, 2004) and *Theories and Practices of American Libraries in the Twenty-First Century* (Beijing Library Press, 2007). He is the author of *Princess Peacock: Tales from the Other Peoples of China* (Libraries Unlimited, 2008), *The Magic Lotus Lantern and Other Tales from the Han Chinese* (Libraries Unlimited, 2006), and co-author of *Celebrate Chinese New Year, Holidays around the World Series* (National Geographic, 2009).

Yuan has been a professor at Western Kentucky University in the Department of Library Public Services since 1997. He is now Special Assistant to the Dean of Libraries, and serves on the board of the Chinese American Librarians Association.

This Is China

The First 5,000 Years

Chapter 1:
Background–The
Land and the People

Běijǐng zhīshi
背景知识

*C*hina's high profile in world history corresponds to its size and huge population, but also (and especially) to the longevity and distinctiveness of Chinese civilization. Ancient China introduced the world to a written language system that is still in use, and to paper, printing, gunpowder, and the compass (the "Four Great Inventions"). The Chinese term "Zhōngguó" 中国, which in English we translate as "China," literally means "Middle Kingdom." The name referred in ancient times to the middle reaches of the Huang (Yellow) River valley. As early as the fifth century BCE, according to *Yǔgòng* 禹贡 (*Tribute of Yu*), a chapter in the Confucian classic *Shàngshū* 尚书 (*Esteemed Documents*), the Chinese subdivided their territory into regions of different geographic and economic features. Gradually the name "Zhongguo" evolved to encompass all the lands under the direct rule of its dynasties. China's imperial borders would expand, contract, and expand again over the centuries—throughout periods of disunity, war, and reunification—to absorb territory occupied by diverse peoples. As the result of the last Chinese Civil War (1945–1949), two political entities emerged that had earlier been considered "one China": the People's Republic of China (PRC), commonly known as "mainland China," and the Republic of China (ROC), which comprises Taiwan and its surrounding islands.

Chapter 1 introduces mainland China's distinctive physical and human geographies, and the ways in which they were inextricably linked. Varied topography—for the most part rugged and harsh in the vast expanse of the west, and temperate and fertile in much of the east—impacted the movement and settlement of China's population over millennia. The size of that population today, historically and still heavily concentrated in the east, is one of the country's most well-known and publicized aspects: the People's Republic of China, home to about 1,330,000,000 people in 2009, is by far the most populous country on Earth. The decimal shorthand for that number, 1.33 billion, tends to downplay its magnitude, since the "point 33" behind the "1" (330

1

million people) exceeds by almost 22 million the U.S. population in 2009. (Simply put, there are a billion more people living in China than in the United States.) The impact of such a huge population is one of China's overriding concerns today: as a sustainable development strategist with the Chinese Academy of Sciences explains, any trifling problem in China can be enormous if multiplied by 1.33 billion, whereas any achievement, however brilliant, will pale if divided by the same figure.

Physical Geography

(Zìrán dìlǐ 自然地理)

The People's Republic of China is one of the largest countries in the world (after Russia and Canada), covering nearly 9.6 million square kilometers, or roughly 3.07 million square miles. Although China is approximately the same size as the United States, a comparison of the two countries' "measurements" depends on several factors: whether PRC claims on territories also claimed by India are valid; where a number of China's ill-defined boundaries are drawn; and how the total size of the United States is calculated. (For China's exact "dimensions" see "Mapping Out China: Some Numbers and Statistics," in the supplementary information to this volume available at www.berkshirepublishing.com.)

China and the United States share similarities other than size: Both are located in the middle latitudes of the Northern Hemisphere. Both have extensive coastlines fronting on middle latitude oceans and seas, although China, unlike the United States, is directly

Thought Experiment

Throughout history the "extreme geography" of western China kept this vast territory isolated from the more hospitable climate and terrain of eastern China. As you read about China's land, its resources, its population—and its history—discuss how this "downside" became an advantage to China, both domestically and internationally.

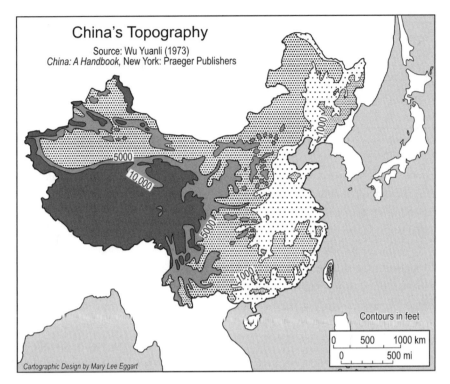

Source: Gregory Veeck, Clifton W. Pannell, Christopher J. Smith, & Yougin Huang. (2007). *China's Geography: Globalization and the Dynamics of Political, Economic, and Social Change*. Lanham, MD: Rowman & Littlefield.

accessible by water only from the east and south. The climate, topography, and soils of southeastern China and the southeastern United States are very much alike. In some ways, the stereotypical notion of the "Wild West" in the early United States as unsettled and remote can be applied to the "frontier" of western China. If China had time zones, there would be four of them, the same as in the continental United States. The Chinese government, however, thinking that one time zone unifies people spread across an enormous territory, has decided that the entire country should run on Beijing time.

Varied Terrain (Dìxíng duōbiàn 地形多变)

China's territory includes a variety of complex landscapes. In the east, along the shores of the Huang (Yellow) Sea and the East China Sea, lie extensive and densely populated alluvial plains, while grasslands occupy the edges of the Inner Mongolian Plateau in the north. To the west, major mountain ranges, including the Himalayas, and high plateaus stand out from the more arid landscapes of the Taklimakan and Gobi deserts. In the

---

Topics for Further Study

Climate and Vegetation

Grasslands

Huang (Yellow) River

Mount Wudang

---

south, the land is dominated by hill country and low mountain ranges. The Chinese coastline is about 18,400 kilometers (about 11,443 miles) along the Bohai Bay, Beibu Bay, East China Sea, Yellow Sea, and South China Sea.

Gregory Veeck, co-author of *China's Geography: Globalization and the Dynamics of Political, Economic, and Social Change*, explains how the rugged terrain of China's western regions, which for three millennia have remained sparsely populated, isolated China from neighboring nations and cultures. (Even in the twenty-first century formidable topography and great distances thwart westward connections with the remainder of Asia.) That spatial isolation, coupled with an inhospitable climate, has given western China a distinct developmental and cultural history when compared with the rest of the country. Throughout the centuries, writes Veeck, China focused on overcoming the challenge of its internal physical geography. That is, China's imperial governments spent considerable time and energy melding its various cultures and regions rather than concentrating on external expansion. Despite easy access to the sea and a huge and powerful naval fleet at its command during the early fifteenth century, China's experience was much different than that of small nations such as England and the Netherlands, whose maritime colonial expansion made them, in their heyday, among the most powerful in the world.

Rivers and Lakes (Héliú yǔ húbó 河流与湖泊)

China has more than 1,500 rivers, each with a drainage basin of at least 1,000 square kilometers (about 386 square miles). (A river's drainage basin, also called a catchment area, is the extent of land on which rainwater or snowmelt flows downhill and is thus "funneled" into the river.) The water flowing along these rivers—more than 2,700 billion cubic meters (95,350 billion cubic feet)—equals 5.8 percent of the world's total. The longest Chinese river is the Yángzǐ 扬子江 (Cháng 长江) in central China, the third longest in the world after the Nile in northeast Africa and the Amazon in South America; its catchment area is about one-fifth the size of China itself. The river, which over centuries cut deep gorges in the countryside, has been prominent in the development of Chinese trade and culture. It is now a vital source of hydroelectric power. Although the Three Gorges Dam on the Yangzi opened in October 2008, building the dam sparked controversy over construction costs, the loss of historic and prehistoric artifacts, the potential environmental impacts of the project, and the displacement of as many as 4 million people.

The Huáng 黄河, China's second largest river, was named for the yellow silt in its waters. Westerners have come to call the Huang "China's sorrow" for the devastation caused by flooding in its surrounding flatlands and farms, but people in China refer to the Huang as "Mother River." Other principal rivers include the Hēilóngjiāng in the northeast, the Pearl in the southeast, and the Láncāng and Yarlung Zangbo the southwest.

China's natural lakes number around 3,000; about 130 cover an area of more than 1,000 square kilometers (about 386 square miles). But due to problems caused by population growth and economic development, China's total lake area has shrunk by about 16,500 square kilometers (about 6,370 square miles) since 1950; an average of twenty lakes vanish each year. Lake Pōyáng, the largest freshwater lake, is home to half a million migratory birds in winter, notably the endangered white crane, although all its wildlife inhabitants are threatened by environmental degradation caused by sand dredging from the Poyang, a mainstay of the local economy. China's largest inland body of saltwater is Qinghai Lake, located 3,205 meters (10,515 feet) above sea level on the Qinghai-Tibetan Plateau. Qinghai Lake is fed by twenty-three rivers and streams, and is home to the Niǎodǎo (Bird Island) sanctuary. To deal with the fact that the lake shrunk by more than 380 square kilometers (about 147 square miles) between 1959 and 2006, a government plan enabled the moving of hotels, restaurants, and other tourist facilities to an area at least 3 kilometers (a little less than two miles) from its banks.

Climate (Qìhòu 气候)

China's climate is as varied as its landscape, ranging from tropical on the island of Hainan in the south to subarctic in Mòhé County in the northeast. From October to March, winds blow from a strong high-pressure system overlaying Siberia and the Mongolia Plateau into China, decreasing in force as they move southward. These conditions cause dry and cold winters in much of the country and a temperature difference of 40°C (72°F) between the north and the south. In the winter, the temperature in China is 5° to 18°C (9 to 32.4°F) lower than that in other countries on the same latitude. In summer, monsoon winds blow into China from the ocean, bringing with them warm and humid air masses and rains. The city of Kūnmíng, located on the Yunnan-Guizhou Plateau, is unique in that it experiences the warmth of spring year round.

Annual precipitation also varies greatly from region to region: as high as 1,500 millimeters (59 inches) along the southeastern coast and as low as 50 millimeters (less than 2 inches) in the northwest, particularly the Tarim Basin.

Vegetation, Cultivation, and Mineral Resources (Kěnzhí yǔ kuàngcáng 垦殖与矿藏)

China's great range of natural vegetation, which includes most types native to the Northern Hemisphere, except of course for varieties found in arctic regions, can be categorized (roughly) by geographic area. Along the southern coast of the country and in Hainan Island, tropical rain forests and other plants indigenous to the tropics thrive, while in the subtropical south and central area broad-leaved evergreens, pines, and many varieties of bamboo are found. In the high mountains of western China and Tibet, alpine and subalpine plant communities abound. At lower western elevations the country holds vegetation common to desert, steppe, savanna, and prairie meadow.

Forestland covers 133.7 million hectares (about 329 million acres) of China's terrain. Most old-growth (coniferous evergreen and deciduous) forests are in the northeast, where Changbai Mountain, designated as an International Biosphere Protection Zone by UNESCO (United Nations Education, Scientific, and Cultural Organization), boasts a wide variety of flora. International support and funding for forest biopreserves in Heilongjiang Province has played a critical role in the protection of these northeastern forests, where major species including conifers (Korean pine, larch, and Olga bay larch) and broadleaves (white birch, oak, willow, elm and northeast China ash) are found. Forests in the northeast were first extensively exploited for commerce beginning in 1949, but since the late 1990s commercial timber operations have gradually shifted to the southern portions of the country, where longer growing seasons

The Dujiangyan Irrigation System in Sichuan, built in 256 BCE, is still in use and intact after the earthquake of May 2008. PHOTO BY RUTH MOSTERN.

double or triple annual production. Trees in the southwest include dragon spruce, fir and Yunnan pine, as well as precious teak, red sandalwood, and camphor trees.

In the eastern part of the country, densely settled for thousands of years, identifying native vegetation can be somewhat difficult for several reasons. For several millennia China's farmers cut and burned trees, shrubs, and grasses in order to clear fields. Thus new species from other parts of China and Asia have been introduced extensively for slope stabilization and forestry, as well as for cultivation. Likewise, because fuel for cooking and heat has been long scarce, especially in northern China, local peasants devastated forests and grasslands in the search for fuel and construction materials. While increasingly stringent logging bans since the late 1990s may protect the forests for posterity, such conservation measures have made unemployment in the north reach levels as high as those in other rural areas of China. Extensive areas of old growth forests also exist in Tibet, western Sichuan, and Yunnan provinces. Most of these areas could be characterized as poor and remote. This isolation, while a major impediment to improving the living standards and economies of such places, Gregory Veeck explains in *China's Geography*, has also protected these forests to an extent not possible in more accessible areas.

For much of its long history, China has been a nation of farmers; agriculture dates from about 10,000 years ago and perhaps even longer. In southeastern and southwestern China, below the Qinling Mountain range that serves as a natural barrier between the drier north and the wetter south, drainage canals permitted early Chinese farmers to irrigate their new fields, and thus to raise rice. Rice grew naturally in shallow water alongside lakes and riverbanks of Southeast Asia, where local gardeners began to harvest it as early as 8000 BCE. Artificial dikes and canals, like those the Chinese built in the Huang River valley, enormously extended the area of suitably shallow water. The Dujiangyan irrigation system in southern China's Sichuan Province (built in the third century BCE along the Min River, one of the longest headwaters of the Yangzi), still functions to regulate the flow of water and to prevent flooding along the fertile Chengdu Plain.

China's great environmental diversity, Veeck points out, allows for a wide variety of agricultural production; it also offers some protection against damage from local or regional natural catastrophes. The summer floods on many of China's rivers in 1998 were the worst in almost fifty years, for instance, but the national summer grain crop was one of the largest on record as conventionally dry interior grain areas recorded unusually high yields. Protected in this way by its sheer size, Veeck writes, China is still able to meet upwards of 95 percent of its citizens' food requirements while producing an ever-expanding variety of different commodities—grains, fruits, vegetables, commercial/industrial crops, and livestock—for export as well as domestic consumption. Indeed, throughout China's long history the importance of providing the nation's people with food has been linked with the political stability of the state.

China's cultivated land comprises about 94.97 million hectares (about 234 million acres), mainly in the Northeast Plain, the North China Plain, the Middle-Lower Yangzi Plain, the Pearl River Delta Plain, and the Sichuan Basin. Because China has a large population, the area of cultivated land per capita is less than 0.08 hectare, or only one-third of the world's average. In the Northeast Plain fertile black soil is ideal for growing wheat, corn, sorghum, soybeans, flax and sugar beets. Wheat, corn, millet, sorghum and cotton thrive in the deep, brown topsoil of the North China Plain, while the many lakes and rivers of the Middle-Lower Yangzi Plain make that area particularly suitable for paddy rice.

Contrary to China's low world ranking in cultivated land per capita, it ranks first in reserves of such rare metal and earth as germanium, tungsten, scandium, ytterbium, and lanthanum. (China is the third-richest country in minerals at large, having about 153 minerals confirmed as of 2000.) Such bountiful supplies illustrate how China's vast mountains and plateaus can be seen as both a blessing and a curse: they have restricted economic development, transportation, and national integration, but the mineral resources they hold are vital for China's continued economic development. China's rich supply of natural resources includes energy sources like coal, petroleum, natural gas, and oil shale. China's coal reserves total 1,007.1 billion tons, mainly distributed in Shanxī Province and Inner Mongolia.

Terraced rice paddies lead to Shan Qiao village in the Hengduan Mountains, Yunnan.
PHOTO BY JOAN LEBOLD COHEN.

Human Geography

(Rénwén dìlǐ 人文地理)

Archaeological evidence of human-made tools found in the Rénzìdòng Cave 人字洞 in Ānhuī Province suggests that the earliest humans in China date to about 2.24 million years ago. Three foraging era (Paleolithic) cultures—lower, middle, and upper—that correspond in general to the evolution of humans, from *Homo erectus* to *Homo sapiens* to *Homo sapiens sapiens* (modern humans), have been discovered at archaeological sites in twenty-seven provinces and autonomous regions of China. Based on paleomagnetic dating of two human incisors, the "Yuánmóu Man" 元谋人 is thought to have lived in Yunnan approximately 1.7 million years ago, although some scholars have reexamined the evidence and now estimate the teeth to be 600,000 to 500,000 years old. Human fossils of "Peking Man," who lived in Zhōukǒudiàn 周口店 to the southwest of modern Běijīng, as well as other remains from that cave site, date from 550,000 to 300,000 to years ago and suggest that the *Homo erecti* population living there made and used simple tools, and most likely knew how to make fire. In the middle foraging era in China (roughly 128,000 to 35,000 years ago), human populations increased, living not only in caves but in camps above ground and near water. The natural environment changed drastically, and depending on the locale—whether the cool and dry north, the temperate grasslands, or the tropical and subtropical forests areas—people engaged in some combination of

Thought Experiment

China's autonomous regions, all of which are located in underdeveloped western and southwestern China, are contested spaces where local ethnic-minority traditions and growing intrusions by the Han Chinese majority have yet to reach a balance. Demands placed on the environment have now shifted dramatically in response to China's changing economy and society. What problems do these regional differences create for China?

Fossil remains from cave sites of Peking Man—his skull is replicated here— suggest that the *Homo erecti* population in China made simple tools. PHOTO BY YAN LI.

hunting and food gathering. They began to make small, well-polished tools as well as refined objects for ornamental purposes. During the upper foraging era in China, which ended about 10,000 years ago, humans evolved to become modern humans, the glacial period peaked, the weather patterns gradually warmed to become what they are today, and tools and objects, whether in stone or in combination with animal horn, bone, or shell, became even more sophisticated and specialized.

Remains discovered at about two thousand excavation sites across China provide evidence of the Yǎngsháo (仰韶) culture, dating from about 5000 to 3000 BCE, one of best-known of the Chinese Neolithic era (8000–5500 BCE), remarkable for its painted red pottery. Yangshao people lived in communities with subterranean and above-ground houses built of wood and earth; they supplemented their millet-based agricultural society by hunting, gathering, and fishing. The Yangshao culture afforded high social status to its women, although men were still the primary holders of economic and political power.

As societies developed the need for governance increased. Historical records, some of which scholars question, as well as archaeological evidence just as controversial, indicate that the Xià 夏 (2100?–1766? BCE) was the first Chinese dynasty. Since then over four hundred monarchs came and went in the following 4,000 years—see chapter 2 for an account of dynasties and imperial governance leading to the birth of modern China in the twentieth century.

Ethnicities (Mínzú 民族)

Hundreds of ethnic groups have existed in China throughout its history. The largest by far is the Hàn 汉, making up slightly more than 91 percent of the total population as of 2010. Over the last three millennia, many previously distinct ethnic groups in China were assimilated into the Han, dramatically expanding the size of its population over time. These assimilations were usually incomplete, however, and vestiges of indigenous languages and cultures are still visible among the Han in different regions of China. As of 2010 there are fifty-five officially recognized ethnic minority groups (shǎoshù mínzú 少数民族) in China, numbering about 110 million people. Taken together, ethnic minority homelands occupy more than half of China, including 90 percent of its border areas, and provide the nation with most of its minerals, forest reserves, animal and meat products, and medicinal herbs. In these homelands, known as "autonomous regions," the indigenous ethnic minorities usually number less than half the total population, however, and in some of these areas (especially the Xīnjiāng Uygur Autonomous Region and the Tibetan Autonomous Region), immigration by Han Chinese is on the rise.

Article 4 of the Constitution of the People's Republic of China (1982) states that all nationalities in the PRC are equal; a 1984 amendment includes a number of provisions to (1) ensure that ethnic minorities have the right to form autonomous organizations and self-governing bodies and to garner support from higher level organizations; (2) that unskilled workers receive training; and (3) that relationships among groups strengthen. Nevertheless, problems remain concerning self-determination and autonomy. The 1978–1979 opening of China's economy to world markets brought prosperity to the nation and fostered a renewal of interest in and respect for ethnic minorities that had disappeared during the Cultural Revolution (1966–1976), but economic policy focused on the eastern coastal areas of China, not the western areas in which most minorities live. Efforts beginning in the 1990s to correct the imbalance between the thriving east and the poorer west have yet to be satisfactorily effective.

For a list of ethnic minorities and their populations (based on mainland China's latest census in 2000), see table 1 in the supplementary information to this volume available at www.berkshirepublishing.com.

Faiths and Philosophies (Zōngjiào 宗教)

China's imperial history reflects the global exchange of religious beliefs and philosophical thinking. Before the seventh century CE people adhered to three main tenets: Confucianism—based on the teachings of Confucius, one of China's first and greatest philosophers—encouraged principles of benevolence (rén 仁), trust (xìn 信), righteousness (yì 义), propriety (lǐ 礼), and knowledge (zhì 智); Daoism, a religion whose followers synthesized the teachings of the philosopher Laozi with disparate beliefs (i.e.,

Confucius 孔夫子

Confucius (551–479 BCE) is China's greatest philosopher. For centuries, his teachings have influenced Chinese thinking about a person's ideal education and the proper way to behave.

Confucius was born in the state of Lu (鲁 in today's Shandong Province) with the family name of Kong (孔) and the given name Qiu (丘), which was stylized as Zhongni (仲尼). He was eventually given the title "Kong the Grand Master" (Kong fuzi 孔夫子), later Latinized as Confucius. He married at nineteen, had two daughters and a son, and held a minor office in Lu. He dedicated his life to teaching, but believed his true calling was to reform the decaying Zhou culture. At the age of fifty-one, Confucius was promoted to magistrate and subsequently to Minister of Justice of Lu. Disillusioned with his ability to change the bureaucracy, Confucius set out five years later with his closest disciples to other states in search of a worthy ruler who would implement his teachings. After almost thirteen years, he returned to Lu to teach. According to traditional Chinese history, he wrote or edited the Five Classics: *Shujing* (书经 *Classic of History*), *Shijing* (诗经 *Classic of Poetry*) *I Ching* (易经 or *Yijing, Classic of Changes*), *Chunqiu* (春秋 *Spring and Autumn Annals*), and *Liji* (礼记 *Classic of Rites*), as well as the now-lost *Classic of Music*.

After his death, Confucius's influence and reputation only grew. By the time of Mencius (371–289 BCE), another famed Chinese philosopher, Confucius was considered a sage. Emperors of the Han dynasty (206 BCE–220 CE) made offerings at his tomb, which became a shrine and later a temple. During the Song dynasty (960–1279), the scholar Zhu Xi streamlined and compiled details of Confucius's life and teachings in the Four Books: *Daxue* (大学 *Great Learning*), *Zhongyong* (中庸 *Doctrine of the Mean*), *Lunyu* (论语 *Analects of Confucius*), and *Mengzi* (孟子 *Mencius*), of which the Analects is the most important.

Confucius was an innovative teacher. His school was open to all serious students, and it transformed aristocratic mores into collective moral values. Confucius emphasized literacy (*wén* 文) and demanded that his students be enthusiastic, serious, and self-reflective. He held that all persons, but especially the ruling class, must develop moral integrity by practicing ritual action (*lǐ* 礼) in order to express humanity (*rén* 仁) and to become a consummate person (*jūnzǐ* 君子). One word that defines his teachings is *shù* (恕), meaning "empathy," which is defined in the *Analects* as "never do to another what you do not desire." With a renewed interest in Confucius in China, his teachings continue to influence many aspects of Chinese culture.

yīn–yáng 阴阳 theory and the benefits of traditional Chinese medicine); and Buddhism (a religion based on goals of achieving wisdom and compassion, and on doing no harm to humans or animals), which came to China from India via central Asia. Traditional ancestral religions, which involved rites, prayers, sacrifices, and festivals that celebrate ancestors as well as land and nature, had a huge impact on Chinese society, and eventually on dynastic politics.

In twenty-first-century China people practice—officially, under control of the state—five religions protected by the constitution: Buddhism, Daoism, Islam, Catholicism, and Protestantism. Belief in polytheistic folk religions that venerate ancestors and emphasize the externalization of reputation (*míng* 名)—the practice of which includes worshiping gods and goddesses of good fortune, fertility, longevity, and safety, among others—is widespread throughout the country, but followers of these faiths, and of Christianity and Islam as well, often experience less "freedom" than Buddhists and Daoists.

Although religious practice is a constitutional right for the populace at large, the Chinese Communist Party requires its members to espouse Marxist atheism. China is wary of any unregulated religious or similar groups and gatherings. Since its official position is separation from foreign creed, any unauthorized or "underground" gatherings—of Vatican loyalists for example—are discouraged or even suppressed. The fate of these Roman Catholics in China apparently depends on improved relationship between China and Vatican, the only state in Europe (as of 2010) that recognizes Taipei (in Taiwan) instead of Beijing as China's legitimate government.

Language (**Yǔyán** 语言)

Today most languages in China, including those spoken by the Han majority and twenty-eight other ethnicities, belong to the Sinitic branch of the Sino-Tibetan language family. The Han people primarily speak Mandarin, the language used by 70 percent of China's population. In 1995, Modern Standard Chinese, based on the Beijing dialect of Mandarin called Pǔtōnghuà (the common language 普通话), was designated as China's national language to foster ease of communication. Han speak seven other dialects—Wú (Shanghainese), Yuè (Cantonese), Xiāng, Gàn, Hakka, Southern Mǐn, and Northern Min—but they are mutually unintelligible.

Ethnic minorities speak about 120 different non-Sinitic languages; the most common include Zhuàng (Thai), Mongolian, Tibetan, Uygur (Turkic), Hmong, and Korean, not all of which exist in written form. These languages belong to the Altaic, Indo-European, South Asian, and South Island families. Many of them face the danger of extinction because, individually, they are known to fewer than a thousand people.

Topics for Further Study

Ethnic Minorities

Historical Geography

Music, Traditional

Religious Practice, Contemporary

Han who work among ethnic minorities are encouraged to learn to speak these languages, and bilingual education programs are becoming increasingly common in China's ethnic autonomous regions. Even so, people must speak Mandarin to advance socially, economically, and politically.

Wényánwén 文言文, or classical Chinese, was the language used as the standard for literature and formal writing in China before the twentieth century, although remnants of the language still survive in the form of idioms, allusions, and expressions. From 650 CE to 1905 social and intellectual life in China had been especially dominated by the rigorous tests known as civil service examinations (kējǔ 科举), a system used to recruit officials based on merit rather than on family or political connections. Because legions of men trained and studied to take these exams (women were excluded), but relatively few achieved the extremely high grade needed to become a court official, men from a number of professions and social ranks, from physicians to merchants to landed gentry, comprised China's literati class. The stress on classical language in literature and Confucian-based philosophies gave the Chinese a unified cultural voice in times of invasion by the Mongols (see discussion of the Southern Sòng dynasty [1127–1279] and the Yuán dynasty [1279–1368] in chapter 2). Vernacular Chinese, or báihuà 白话, a written standard based on the Mandarin dialect, was first popularized in Míng-dynasty (1368–1644) novels and was later adopted with significant modification as the more colloquial, national vernacular during the Republican era of the early twentieth century. When China's last imperial government (the Qīng, 1644–1911/12) lost control of the educational system in 1904, Chinese intellectuals were ready for this new unifying voice, one that spoke the language of nationalism and reform.

The concept of "chronological geography" as a way to approach Chinese history reached its zenith during the Qing. (Scientific or "modern" geography did not reach China from the West until about 1910.) Over centuries Confucian scholars had developed a systematically arranged geographical order by which to record and preserve imperial ideology; the Qing, clinging to traditional values until the bitter end, reconstructed such historical treatises sponsored by past dynasties, paying special attention to how descriptions of administrative systems, road networks, and water systems changed over time, and to verifying the locations of key historical events and settlements. Chapter 2—which begins with an account of China's mythological origins, moves through its earliest cultures and states, and goes on to cover the entire period of China's imperial empire—continues the story of China's history, its land, and its people.

Chapter 2: From Prehistory to the End of the Empire

Shǐqián zhì mòdài wángcháo
史前至末代王朝

According to Chinese mythology, the Earth was created in the midst of chaos. Within that chaos nested a huge primordial egg. In that egg grew a giant named Pán Gǔ 盘古; in some versions of the myth he is said to be a primal deity and the offspring of Yīn 阴 and Yáng 阳, the two vital forces of the universe. After eighteen thousand years Pan Gu broke through the egg's shell (some stories say he used an axe, others describe how the shell just cracked). From the opaque yolk that spilled out, Earth took shape under his feet; the clear "white" of the egg rose to form the sky. Pan Gu continued to grow, always holding the sky above the Earth. After another eighteen thousand years, thinking that Earth and sky were secure in their positions, Pan Gu laid down to rest one night and then died from exhaustion. Parts of his body became elements of the universe; his bones turned into the mountains, his blood flowed and became the rivers, his breath the moisture of the air, and his hair the vegetation. Even the lice on his body, myth tells us, morphed into animal life.

Chinese myth attributes the creation of human life to Nǚ Wā 女娲, a goddess whose lower body was like a snake's. Living on the Earth after its separation from the heavens, she was lonely; after looking at her reflection in a pool of water she decided to sculpt a tiny copy of herself—which would become the first human—from mud. But the process was slow, and Nǚ Wā was impatient, so she dipped a vine into mud and shook it, thereby splattering the mud and turning the multitude of droplets into a whole population of human beings. To prevent this new species from dying off, she paired them so they could reproduce.

Civilizations, of course, depend on more than procreation to survive. Chinese myth credits Sānhuáng-Wǔdì 三皇五帝 for creating a succession of eight legendary sage-emperors and culture heroes who instructed the ancient Chinese in communicating with one another, finding sustenance, and fabricating clothing and shelter.

15

Dates	Dynasty	Pronunciation	People, Places, and Things
2100?–1766? BCE	Xia Dynasty	"Zeeah"	Real or Legendary?
1766–1045 BCE	Shang Dynasty	"Shahng"	Ancestor Worship and Oracle Bones
1045–256 BCE	Zhou Dynasty	"Joe"	Bronze, Jade, and Confucius
221–206 BCE	Qin Dynasty	"Chin"	Terracotta Soldiers
206 bce–220 CE	Han Dynasty	"Hahn"	Paper, Porcelain, and the Silk Roads
220?–589? CE	Southern and Northern Dynasties		China's "Dark Ages"
618–907 CE	Tang Dynasty	"Tahng"	Poetry and Literature
907–960 CE	Five Dynasties and Ten Kingdoms		Short-Lived Reigns
960–1279	Song Dynasty	"Soong" (like "woo")	Markets, Paper Money, and the Abacus
1125–1234	Jurchen Jin Dynasty	"Jurchen Jin"	Cavalry Warfare
1279–1368	Yuan Dynasty	"Yoo-EN"	Mongol Rule
1368–1644	Ming Dynasty	"Ming"	Building the Great Wall
1644–1911/12	Qing Dynasty	"Ching"	Manchu Rule

Chinese mythology dates back some four thousand years—to just about the same time that the tribal people known as the Xià 夏 were said to first thrive in northern China—but the versions of the myths above took roughly two thousand years to formulate before they were written down. We can imagine how stories about the Xia might have changed as they passed from generation to generation, just like the stories of myth. (Did Pan Gu really have an axe with him in the egg, or did the shell just crack?) Is it surprising, then, that China's earliest dynasty is the subject of much scholarly contention?

"Dynasties Song"

Singing "Dynasties Song" to the tune of "Frère Jacques" is a good way to remember the major Chinese dynasties in chronological order.

Shang, Zhou, Qin, Han
Shang, Zhou, Qin, Han
Sui, Tang, Song
Sui, Tang, Song
Yuan, Ming, Qing, Republic
Yuan, Ming, Qing, Republic
Mao Zedong
Mao Zedong

Source: Courtesy of the teachers on the College Board AP–World History Listserv legendary or real

Xia Dynasty: Real or Legendary?

Xià cháo: shǐqián yǔ chuánshuō
夏朝: 史前与传说
2100?–1766? BCE

he Xia dynasty, dated by some scholars to approximately 2100 BCE, is the earliest Chinese dynasty to be described in ancient historical records. Those records, however, were first transmitted through oral traditions such as storytelling, song, and drama, and the earliest was not written down for some two thousand years. Although archeologists discovered artifacts in 1928 to support the existence of the Xia, the evidence did not correlate to the historical records. No wonder modern scholars have debated, and still do, whether the Xia dynasty was legendary or real.

Xia Dynasty: Debatable Dates

The Chinese used to refer to the Ming dynasty's Yongle Dadian *as the "greatest event in cultural history." No longer. The Xia Shang Zhou Chronology Project (XSZCP) has usurped the 11,095-volume encyclopedia's top position. The XSZCP, winner of the PRC's "Ten Great Scientific Progress Awards," began in 1996 as a taxpayer-funded scholarly collaboration to develop an agreed-upon timeline for one of the most contentious chronologies of China's history.*

Stories of the Xia, handed down from oral tradition, were eventually chronicled in annals such as the first century BCE *Records of the Grand Historian*, an earlier text—*Bamboo Annals* (written on bamboo slips, interred with the Wei king circa 296 BCE, and rediscovered in 281 CE), and a traditional chronology based on calculations by Liu Xin (c. 46 BCE–23 CE), an astronomer and historian. The dates given for the Xia in these histories vary to a considerable degree.

The aptly named "Skeptical School" of early Chinese history, founded in the 1920s, seriously questioned the veracity of these traditional tomes, noting that over time oral histories had been embellished to flesh out missing details. With an increase in archaeological excavation in the 1920s, scientists developed methods of dating to establish chronologies, and thus supplemented textual interpretation, whether the "text" was written on bronze, oracle bones, bamboo, or paper.

Some seventy years later, enter XSZCP, a multidisciplinary effort commissioned by the PRC in 1996; two hundred scholars were asked to propose chronological frameworks for Xia, the early Shang, the late Shang, and the Western Zhou dynasties. The report, published in 2000, determined that the Xia dynasty dated from 2070 to 1600 BCE. The Chinese government officially accepted the report, but it caused considerable controversy when results were announced overseas.

Although the word "exact" appears only once in the project's overview, scholars found plenty to argue about; both Chinese and Western historians let tempers fly. The *New York Times* reported that Stanford University professor David Nivison claimed he would "tear [the report] into pieces." The Chinese media portrayed the international criticizers as "imperialists" and "hostile forces," while some in the West countered that the project was politically motivated and nationalistic.

Since those initial outbursts both sides have participated in three academic conferences and have debated face to face, but the intensity of such encounters is still reported as fierce. A large part of the controversy involves methodology, which can be as different

---

Xia Dynasty: Debatable Dates (*Continued*)

as carbon dating or interpreting the astronomical data reported in the *Bamboo Annals*. An article by Professor Nivison's, published in the spring 1995 edition of the journal *Early China News* and presented at a 1997 conference in Boulder, Colorado, reveals some of the complex problems involved in coming to terms with dates. The paper can be accessed on the Internet at the source below.

Source: David V. Nivision. (1997). The Riddle of the *Bamboo Annals*. Retrieved December 6, 2009, from http://www.stanford.edu/~dnivison/rdl-aos.html

---

The Xia period links late Neolithic cultures with the urban civilization of the first historically documented dynasty, the Shāng 商 (1766–1045 BCE). The Xia had villages and urban centers, but they were primarily an agrarian people. Their pottery and bronze implements continue to assist historians in developing more definitive chronologies. During the Xia dynasty the major crafts included jade carvings and cast bronze vessels (some of the vessels were embellished with jade). The Xia also devised a calendar system that incorporated lunar and solar movements. Excavations in 1959 at Èrlǐtóu 二里头 (in Yǎnshī 偃师 County, Hénán Province), uncovered what appears to have been a capital of the Xia dynasty, and although no historical record of it exists, archaeological evidence (including radiocarbon dating) demonstrated that the inhabitants were the direct ancestors of the Lóngshān 龙山 culture and predecessors of the Shang.

Traditional Chinese histories contend that the Xia dynasty was founded when a ruler named Shùn 舜 ceded his throne to his minister, Yǔ 禹, because he believed him to be the "perfect civil servant." Yu was esteemed by his people for organizing the construction of canals and dikes along all the major rivers, thus eliminating the devastation of annual flooding. But before his death Yu passed power to his son Qǐ 启 and set the precedent for dynastic rule, or the hereditary system, which put family and clan in political and economic control. Rulers often performed as shamans, communicating with spirits for guidance, and the ruling families employed elaborate and dramatic rituals to confirm their political power.

Fifteen descendants of Qi inherited the throne after his death. Several, such as Shàokāng 少康 and Huái 槐, made important contributions to Chinese society, but three were tyrannical emperors: Tàikāng 太康, Kǒngjiǎ 孔甲, and Jié 桀. The Xia dynasty ended under the reign of Jie, whose dictatorial and extravagant ways caused a popular revolt under the leadership of Tāng 汤, the leader of the Shang tribe, who overthrew the Xia and established his own dynasty in 1766 BCE.

Shang Dynasty: Ancestor Worship and Oracle Bones

Shāng cháo: jìzǔ yǔ jiǎgǔwén
商朝: 祭祖与甲骨文
1766–1045 BCE

*I*n the early twentieth century the Shang dynasty posed the same problem for historians as the Xia: no excavated cities or written records existed from the period to verify later chronicles of its history. Not until the late 1920s, when archaeologists uncovered some bone fragments in northern China near the Shang capital at Ānyáng 安阳 in Henan Province, was the first tangible evidence of the dynasty documented. These fragments, which came from the shoulder blades of oxen and the shells of turtles, were just like the so-called dragon bones that nineteenth-century Chinese pharmacists had been grinding up and selling for medicinal purposes, often as a remedy for malaria—most likely people had been finding them for years in random locations and at far-flung sites. The excavated bones were remarkable, just like the dragon bones, for being inscribed with strange glyphs, the precursors of Chinese characters. But their significance, as oracle bones of the Shang, had never been realized before the discovery at Anyang.

Chinese during the Shang dynasty used oracle bones (*jiǎgǔwén* 甲骨文), so named because of the markings inscribed on them, to aid in divination. (By the end of the dynasty the practice became the exclusive privilege of royalty.) Someone would write a question on a bone, or ask for a prediction about the future—*would the next military campaign be a success, what were the prospects for the upcoming royal hunt, is the king in good health*—and then the diviner (oracle) would place a burning-hot bronze tool against the bone until little cracks appeared. The oracle would then interpret the cracks to answer the question. Records from *jiǎgǔwén* dating to the Shang, along with inscriptions etched on bronze vessels (*jīnwén* 金文), cover only the reigns of the last nine kings, from Wǔ Dīng 武丁, said to have held the throne from 1198 to

---

Topics for Further Study

Anyang

Archaeology and Paleontology

Oracle Bones

Religion, Folk

1189 BCE, up to Dì Xīn 帝辛, who died around 1045 BCE. Many oracle-bone inscriptions date to the early part of the next dynasty, the Zhōu 周 (1045–256 BCE).

Nearly twenty-five thousand inscribed pieces were excavated from Anyang between 1928 and 1937; they included more than twenty-two thousand turtle shells and some twenty-two hundred bones. The excavations resumed in 1950; the largest totaled more than five thousand inscribed pieces. About 80 percent of some 4,500 characters used in the oracle-bone inscriptions are recognizable; through their interpretations, scholars themselves have divined much about Shang daily life—the farming methods and techniques for domesticating animals, the treatment of medical conditions, the sophisticated legal system, and the mastery of textile production, for instance.

Religious Ritual and State Power (Zōngjiào yíshì yǔ guójiā zhèngquán 宗教仪式与国家政权)

The Shang ruled through an essentially feudal system based on clan birthright and perpetuated by the cult worship of royal Shang ancestors. At least by the end of the dynasty the king, in his role as the sole interpreter of the oracle-bone messages, acted as head shaman. The capital city of the empire moved several times, as the king regularly marked and claimed his empire by performing ceremonial acts at sacred mountains located at the four cardinal directions on the boundaries of his realm. His political authority was strengthened in the state worship of the royal ancestral line. The Shang ancestors, in return, were believed to provide a beneficial influence on the state.

At the royal residence in Anyang, enormous tombs have been uncovered that reveal such practices as human and animal sacrifice, the ritual burial of chariots, and the ceremonial use of vessels and oracle bones. In order to have enough materials for these ceremonies, the central court of the Shang had to take control of the region's natural resources. Mining was a particularly important industry, and Chinese metal-casting techniques were the most highly developed in the world at the time. A huge bronze foundry covering an area of over 9,290 square meters (100,000 square feet) has been discovered at the Miáopǔběi 苗圃北 site south of Anyang, revealing some of the most remarkable of Bronze Age material culture.

Another important archeological settlement named Zhèngzhōu 郑州 exists, with artifacts dating from the middle period of the Shang dynasty, directly beneath the modern city of that name in Henan. Evidence shows that agricultural lands were referred to as the "Shang's land," which implies that a large portion of the crops were intended to be collected by the state.

Influence of the Shang (Shāngcháo de yǐngxiǎng 商朝的影响)

At the height of its power, Shang influence extended over a remarkable range. Over five hundred sites that were connected culturally to the Shang, although not necessarily politically, have been found in areas that together would cover much of twenty-first-century China.

The Shang's influence did not end when the Zhou succeeded it in 1045 BCE. Its practice of ancestor worship would influence the way China was ruled for centuries to come. Other Shang traditions that carried on were the patrimonial system of passing on political power, elaborate burial rituals, and the use of fortunetelling as a way of deciding how to govern. One development of the Shang that reverberated through Chinese history was the advancement in metallurgy. Another was the beginning of writing, as etched on the bones and shells that appeared in pharmacist's shops more than three thousand years later.

Zhou Dynasty: Bronze, Jade, and Confucius

Zhōu cháo: qīngtóng, yù, Kǒngzǐ
周朝: 青铜、玉、孔子
1045–256 BCE

*T*he transition from one Chinese dynasty to the next was rarely straightforward, and struggles between competing states of varying power and influence during individual dynasties were common. Such strife, internal and external, characterized the Zhou, the longest dynasty in China's history.

Its nearly eight-hundred-year reign is divided into two periods: the Western Zhou (西周 1045–771 BCE) and the Eastern Zhou (东周 770–221 BCE). The Eastern Zhou is further divided into the Spring and Autumn (Chūnqiū 春秋) Period (770–476 BCE) and the Warring States (Zhànguó 战国) Period (475–221 BCE).

The original Zhou nation rose up in the Wèi River valley in Shaanxi (Shǎnxī 陕西). Oracle-bone records dating from the last stages of the Shang dynasty suggest that the Shang at times considered the Zhou group an enemy and at other times a tribute-paying subject. By around 1045 BCE, the Zhou had built a coalition of partners, including states that had been Shang subjects in northern Henan Province, and they destroyed Shang power in the region. The Zhou nation, founded by kings Wén 文 and Wǔ 武, was traditionally considered to foster humane treatment of its conquests and subjects, and to operate a system of utopian agrarian government. The establishment of the Zhou dynasty might have been the first case in Chinese history where the right to rule was based on an ethical justification instead of raw power.

Mandate of Heaven (Tiānmìng 天命)

In texts compiled centuries later, this shift in power from Shang to Zhou was attributed to (and would then be called) the Mandate of Heaven. According to this concept, divine power could deem one king or group unfit to rule—in this case the increasingly corrupt and immoral Shang dynasty—and thus sanction a takeover by another more suitable (i.e., moral) ruler. By the eighth century BCE the Zhou coup was mythologized as a heroic military conquest commanded by heaven and carried out by the king.

By the Hàn 汉 period (206 BCE –220 CE), the *tiānmìng* concept was considered evidence that changes in political power mirrored shifts in a system of natural forces; a ruler's right to inherit power depended on keeping the favor of a higher power. The Mandate of Heaven theory became a permanent part of Chinese political thought.

Thought Experiment

The Mandate of Heaven depended on four basic principles: (1) that the right to rule is granted by heaven; (2) that there can only be one ruler because there is only one heaven; (3) that the right to rule is based on ruling fairly, justly, and wisely; and (4) that the right to rule is not limited to one dynasty. What were the advantages and disadvantages, do you think, for a dynasty that claimed the right to rule?

Later Chinese reformers, all the way up until the end of the last Chinese dynasty, used it to frighten corrupt rulers.

Western Zhou and Prosperity
(Xīzhōu de fánróng 西周的繁荣)

Under the Shang, succession to the throne had passed from brother to brother, but the Zhou established the principle that successors should come from the next generation. The Zhou lineage ruled from the capital Zōngzhōu 宗州 (or Hàojīng 鎬京), located close to their ancestral burial grounds (near modern-day Xī'ān in Shaanxi Province). Over the next two centuries the Zhou rulers consolidated their power through military coercion and trade. They focused on controlling the resources essential to the tribute system of gift giving and award that they inherited from the Shang. Cowrie shells, bronze, and jade, all considered valuable in Shang religion, continued to be important to the Zhou. Although the Zhou initially worshiped the Shang spirits, by the mid-tenth century BCE their own ancestors had become icons of worship. The Zhou rewarded their subjects with sacrificial vessels, ritual clothing, wine, and lands suitable for food production. In return, gift recipients used these items to present mortuary feasts to the Zhou ancestral spirits. The sophistication of Zhou bronze vessels, carved jade, and musical instruments shows that the dynasty, the last one of

---

Zhou dynasty spade-shaped money, cast from bronze, was hollow-handled and smaller than a real digging tool. PHOTO BY JOAN LEBOLD COHEN.

the Bronze Age, had control over resources and production in regions well outside their homeland. At the height of Zhou influence, during the late tenth to the late ninth centuries BCE, the Zhou had power over a network spanning the following modern-day regions: west into Gānsù Province, northeast

Topics for Further Study

Ancestor Worship

Confucian Sites at Qufu

Jade

Zhou Dynasty

to Běijīng, southwest into Sìchuān Province, east into Shandong Province, and south into Hubei Province beyond the Yángzǐ (Cháng) River.

After two successful two centuries of rule, the Zhou state began to decline. One reason may be that a political and economic system based on exchanging materials to ensure the ritual worship of ancestors is not the most efficient. In 771 BCE, as competing states grew in power, the Zhou elite fled east to the city of Chéngzhōu 成州 (or Luòyì 洛邑), located near modern-day Luòyáng 洛阳 in Henan Province.

Eastern Zhou and Philosophy (Dōngzhōu de zhéxué 东周的哲学)

The entire Eastern Zhou era, including the Spring and Autumn (770–476 BCE) period and the Warring States (475–221 BCE) period, is characterized by larger states annexing smaller ones, so that by the third century BCE only a few states remained. During the nearly three-hundred-year Spring and Autumn period, the Zhou rulers were puppets of various former tribute states—Jìn 晋 to the north; Zhèng 郑 to the south; and Qí 齐 to the east—that alternately competed for control and moral authority. The thinking of Chinese philosophers during the Zhou focused on finding the best way to success, and thus contributed to dynastic, political decision making. (Although finding the way [dào 道] applies to many Chinese philosophies, it is most often associated in the West with Daoism, a legacy of the Zhou.)

Some scholars consider the birth of Confucius in 551 BCE in the state of Lǔ 鲁 the most significant event of the Eastern Zhou period. His influence still resounds in Chinese thinking some twenty-five hundred years later. Confucius believed that the Zhou had lost the ways of its founders, Wen and Wu, and he strove to revive the values they embraced. For the state to be governed by moral virtue rather than coercive law, Confucius thought, an individual must be instructed in moral development and virtues. His focus on filial piety reinforced that ideal; a child loyal to his father and family would become a loyal minister of the state. Confucius's most basic philosophy included five virtues: proper rituals (lǐ 礼); human kindness (rén 仁); trustworthiness (xìn 信) in all people, but especially in state officials; correct standards of rightness (*yì* 义); and moral wisdom (*zhì* 智). Adhering to these virtues would result in a well-rounded individual and peace in the empire.

The two foremost philosophical schools in Warring States times were those of the Confucians (Rújiā 儒家) and the Mohists (Mòjiā 墨家), a group founded by Mòzǐ 墨子 (c. 480–c. 390 BCE). Confucians, with their hierarchy of concern that placed one's family and elders before society, could not accept Mozi's idea of "love for everyone" (*jiān'ài* 兼爱), by which he meant that equal concern for each person was the unifying principle of morality. Both groups, however, sometimes came into conflict with their royal patrons. Confucians believed that advisors, however loyal, should argue with their rulers in the attempt to prevent them from doing something wicked or foolish. Mohists believed that man's desire for wealth was the root of all suffering, and they would actively disrupt campaigns of conquest to keep their warlords from preying on their neighbors. Understandably, Mohists didn't have nearly as much influence in the courts of power throughout China's history.

Other philosophies sprang up that were more appreciated by rulers who were looking to justify their exercise of power. Political philosophers such as Hán Fēi 韩非 (d. 233 BCE) created an ideal of statecraft called Legalism (Fǎjiā 法家) that relied on standardized laws, bureaucratic systems, and unfailing obedience to standards of reward and punishment. A book known as *The Art of War* (*Sūnzǐ bīngfǎ* 孙子兵法) also appeared, supposedly authored by a fifth-century sage named Sūnzǐ (or Sun Tzu) 孙子, offering tough advice to political and military leaders. Overall, this period in China was a time of incredible development in ancient and enduring thought, comparable to ancient Greece, which around the mid-Zhou era was also producing such thinkers as Socrates, Plato, and Aristotle. But while Greek philosophers focused on abstract truths, the Chinese sought the best ways in which to live a prosperous life.

The philosophy of Daoism developed in south China from ancient shamanistic practices; it emphasized finding value and purpose in life—and doing so by connecting to nature, often through meditative practice and breathing techniques. Some scholars date the foundational text of Daoism, the *Lǎozǐ* 老子 (or *Dàodéjīng* 道德经, *The Way and its Power*), to the sixth century BCE; its alleged author, a man named Lǎodān 老聃 (Lǎozǐ 老子 or Lǐ Ěr 李耳), was said to have once met and conferred with Confucius. Other scholars challenge the historical authenticity of Laozi's life and believe the work to be a compilation of texts written from the fourth to the third centuries BCE by a variety of authors. The *Laozi*, translated today into many languages, is a set of eighty-one poems (chapters) which include now-famous sayings such as "repay ill will with beneficence" and "a journey of a thousand miles begins with the first step."

The *Laozi* advised rulers to govern the state by cultivating connections to the forces of nature; it saw the *dao* (the way) as ultimate reality, the source from which all things, even the deities, arise—but as a "force" that exerts no control over the things it generates. Chapters 37 and 38, for example, instructed rulers to behave like the *dao*: Although the Way does not interfere, through it everything is done (37). Superior power does not emphasize its power and thus is powerful; inferior power never forgets its power and thus is powerless (38).

Following the many strands of Chinese history from the sixth century BCE onward will show just how much the philosophies sparked by two great Zhou-era thinkers, and refined and modified by their followers and disciples, became thoroughly interwoven into the lives of China's leaders and its people: Confucius, who believed that people could be virtuous and upright if they were educated to be so, and also if they followed tradition; and Laozi—whether real (or mythologized and deified, as his figure was by some during the Han dynasty)—who was more concerned with humankind's ability to live naturally and in harmony with the world.

During the Warring States times, several processes that had begun in the Spring and Autumn period intensified: a decline in centralized power, the rise of warlike and expansionist states; and a decrease in the number of independent states, as the weakest were taken over by the strongest. "Agriculture and war" became a popular slogan (much like the twentieth-century U.S. slogan "guns and butter," that was used in debates about government spending on defense versus the production of civilian goods); rulers realized the necessity of having both a healthy economy and a mighty army. War itself changed from a ritualized competition between educated aristocrats (as in the Spring and Autumn period) to a lawless and bloody struggle between large armies of infantry. The struggle among various peoples continued to the end of the Warring States period. In 256 BCE, the last Zhou king, who was by this time nothing more than a figurehead, was finally deposed.

During the Warring States period, an important but often underestimated figure, Xúnzǐ 荀子 (c. 300–230 BCE), emerged. Considering himself a follower of Confucius, he helped consolidate the Confucian tradition in his time. Xunzi is considered by some to rank third among Chinese philosophers after Confucius and Xunzi's own rival Mencius 孟子 (c. 371–c. 289 BCE). Mencius held that people were good by nature, while Xunzi argued that they needed a rigid hierarchical social structure, constrained by tradition and the threat of punishment, to prevent them from following their naturally evil tendencies. He did believe, however, as did Confucius, that people have the capacity to learn to be morally upright and good.

During the Zhou era the rulers began to rethink their approach to governing their territories. The raising, training, and supplying of a massive army caused all sort of logistical problems, and rulers willing to exploit their resources remained center stage in the theater of war. The state became a vast production ground of people and munitions, maintained by an efficient and organized administration and serving a single king, to whom the entire population owed unquestioning allegiance. Kinship ties, ritual obligations, and traditional practice, the most significant considerations guiding human action in earlier times, were now subordinated to the material requirements of the "warring state." In this manner the imperial model of Chinese statecraft was being forged even before the establishment of the empire itself. The governments of the Qín and Han (206 bce–220 ce) dynasties were largely based on the precedents of the Warring States.

Qin Dynasty: Terracotta Soldiers

Qín cháo: Bīngmǎ yǒng
秦朝: 兵马俑
221–206 BCE

*D*uring the brief fifteen years of its reign, the Qin, China's first imperial dynasty, unified the country with a centralized administration and a model of government that subsequent emperors followed for years. The Qin rulers achieved their successes, however, by harsh, totalitarian acts that hastened their dynasty's fall.

The Qin state (as distinguished from the dynasty) was among the new powers that arose in China during the Warring States period. Living in the present-day province of Shaanxi among the nomadic tribes in the west of China, the Qin people had long been fierce warriors. Their ability to make weapons was facilitated by the wealth of iron ore found in their region. In the middle of the fourth century bce, a scholar and politician named Shāng Yāng 商鞅 (d. 338 bce) gained the favor of the Qin ruler and set about to reform the Qin state. He abolished feudalism, gave land to the peasants, taxed them, and introduced a law code that favored no particular class. Shang Yang was one of the earliest to put into practice the philosophy of Legalism (Fǎjiā 法家), which emphasized that rulers should have absolute power and should govern with the help of a strict law code.

Topics for Further Study

Legalist School

Mausoleum of Qin Shi Huangdi

Mount Tai

Terracotta Soldiers

The "First Sovereign Emperor" (Shǐ Huángdì 始皇帝)

The rise of the Qin state culminated in the years after 260 BCE, by which time only seven large states were left in the struggle for supremacy. The thirteen-year-old Yíng Zhèng 嬴政 (c. 259–210 BCE) came to the throne in 245 BCE; seven years later he instigated a palace coup to depose the regent who had ruled in his name. Between 230 and 221 BCE the Qin annihilated their rivals. By 221 BCE Zheng had unified all the states that had emerged from the feudal rule of the once-mighty Western Zhou dynasty. Zheng, having survived various assassination attempts, most notoriously one by the folk hero Jīng Kē 荆轲, proclaimed himself "Shi Huangdi" 始皇帝 (First Sovereign Emperor). A new dynasty was born.

Shi Huangdi was a controversial figure in history. On the one hand, he unified the country by standardizing such things as weights, currency, and measures. He ordered a canal and national roadway system to be built. He reformed the writing system by creating a new style called *xiǎozhuàn* 小篆 (small seal script) to be used throughout his empire. To defend the country against nomads from central Asia, he had laborers build walled fortifications, much of them connecting older earthen walls, eventually to become the Great Wall of China.

But such massive undertakings, achieved in a few years' time, required harsh, repressive laws and policies. Overworked peasants had to serve not only as agricultural workers, but also as soldiers and builders. Prison sentences and maiming punishments were commonly handed out to those who dissented or just happened to gain the emperor's disapproval. Shi Huangdi feared the power of opposing ideas. In 213 BCE, he ordered that all texts not on the subjects of divination, medicine, forestry, and agriculture be burned; only a single copy of each of the offending volumes was held in the imperial library. (Unfortunately, this library was itself burned to the ground by the invading Han forces in 206 BCE.) To end dissension, Shi Huangdi is said to have had 460 scholars buried alive, although this has not been proven.

Shi Huangdi's great obsession was attaining eternal life. He sent thousands of youths to search for the islands of immortality rumored to exist in the East China

Sea. He employed alchemists to manufacture medicines that would increase longevity. Fearful of his enemies, Shi Huangdi often moved around in a network of tunnels built to connect his palaces. He undertook long journeys to sacred Mount Tai, where he performed sacrificial rituals in the hopes of gaining immortality. He died in 210 BCE upon returning from one of these expeditions. Ironically, the cause of death was said to have resulted from ingesting mercury-based concoctions that, his alchemists declared, held the key to eternal life.

The Rapid Fall of the Qin (Qín wángcháo de xùsù bēngtā 秦王朝的迅速崩塌)

Upon Shi Huangdi's death a struggle for power broke out in the court, primarily involving a eunuch, Zhào Gāo 赵高, and an adviser, Lǐ Sī 李斯. Shi Huangdi's eldest son, the heir apparent, was tricked into committing suicide, and the title of emperor was conferred on a younger son, known as the Second Emperor (reigned 210–207 BCE). He ended his short and turbulent reign by also taking his life. Rule then passed to a young boy, known as the child-emperor. The young emperor surrendered to the emerging Han dynasty in 206 BCE, but was nevertheless killed. With the destruction of the capital the dramatic fifteen-year rule of the Qin ended.

Shi Huangdi was buried just east of the modern-day city of Xī'ān. Judging from the part of the imperial tomb excavated so far, it is apparent that the complex was planned as the final resting place of a man whose life would be continuing on a grand scale. The dimensions are impressive. The complex is 515 meters (0.31 mile) north to south and 485 meters (0.26 mile) east to west. The mausoleum itself, enclosed by a thick outer wall with a tower at each corner, is divided into an east vault and a west vault, of which the former has been largely uncovered. Archeologists in the east vault have found royal chariots and horses sculpted in bronze and, most famously in 1974, an army of some seven thousand life-sized terracotta figures representing the imperial guard, cavalry, infantry, and chariot drivers. Each figure was sculpted wearing the uniform and carrying the weapons appropriate to his branch of service; remarkably, each face was individually molded. The figures were lined up in processional formation, as if setting out on a military campaign; the army presumably was to act as Shi Huangdi's escort and protector. In the west vault, scholars believe, an equal numbers of figures remain buried.

Archaeological excavations of the future will be able to test the accuracy of the description of the mausoleum provided by China's first great historian, Sīmǎ Qiān 司马迁 (145–86? BCE). Writing during the Han dynasty (206 BCE–220 CE), Sima observed that the massive and elaborate tomb was under construction from 245 to 210 BCE, that

In the excavation pit housing Shi Huangdi's mausoleum, terracotta cavalry, infantry, and chariot drivers remain on guard. PHOTO BY ROBIN CHEN.

is, from when Zheng became king of the Qin state at age thirteen until the end of his life. Many laborers literally were worked to death building the tomb, and (according to Sima's account) all surviving laborers were buried with the emperor. Sima described a huge central chamber with a ceiling studded with pearls and other precious stones to represent the sun, moon, and stars; snaking across the floor (the Earth), mercury "replicas" of the Yangzi and Huáng (Yellow) rivers flowed into a miniature ocean also made of mercury, the metal believed to have such great regenerative powers. Whale oil, the longest-burning fuel at the time, provided light. Within this and other chambers of the compound—which represented palaces, temples, and offices—armed crossbows were set, primed to fire on any intruders from this world.

这 就 是 中 国

Han Dynasty: Paper, Porcelain, and the Silk Roads

Hàn cháo: zàozhǐ, cíqì, huǒyào, Sīchóuzhīlù

汉朝: 造纸、瓷器、 丝绸之路

206 BCE–220 CE

*A*fter the short-lived Qin regime, the Han ruled China for four centuries, governing one of the most successful empires in the world at that time. The Han dynasty marked a period of political consolidation, military and economic expansion, invention, agricultural prosperity, and empire building in China.

Han dynasty is divided into two periods: the Former, or Western, Han (206 BCE–23 CE) had its capital in Cháng'ān 长安; the Latter, or Eastern, Han (25–220 CE) moved its capital to the east at Luòyáng 洛阳. The dynastic succession between the Former and the Latter was interrupted by a period of non-Han rule (from 9 to 23 CE) that was eventually overthrown by those opposed to its radical ideas and reforms.

Han Beginnings (Hàn cháo de xīngqǐ 汉朝的兴起)

The Han dynasty was founded in 206 BCE when a military commander named Xiàng Yǔ 项羽 led a group of insurgents in a skirmish that resulted in the Qin monarch's death. Four years later Liú Bāng 刘邦 (256–195 BCE) ascended to the throne; he was the first commoner to lead a dynasty in imperial China, and some scholars prefer to date the Han to 202 BCE, the beginning of Liu Bang's rule. (When Han sovereigns took office they were identified by their personal names and then posthumously assigned a reign name preceded by "Han." Liu Bang thus became known as Hàn Gāozǔ 汉高祖, or, to use the convenient Western descriptor, Emperor Gaozu.) During his rule Gaozu got rid of the brutal laws and heavy taxes of the Qin but kept its basic system of governing. He established a civil bureaucracy, recruiting officials through recommendation and examination, which would support imperial rule in the ten feudal states eventually consolidated under the Han.

Several emperors who succeeded Gaozu followed his policies of requiring imperial subjects to supply corvée (forced labor, often in lieu of wages) and to pay taxes. In a peaceful time, the economy of the country grew. After 154 BCE, when the court defeated a revolt staged by seven kingdoms, the authority of the central government was further established.

An Empire Expanded and Interrupted
(Wángcháo kuòzhāng yǔ zhǐbù 王朝扩张与止步)

Emperor Wǔdì 武帝 (Wu Di, 156–87 BCE) expanded central power by imposing state monopolies on salt and iron. He proclaimed Confucianism the state ideology, and established a Confucian imperial university to train officials. The Han dynasty's armies were able to advance to the northeast into present-day Korea, to the southeast into Vietnam, and to the northwest as far as Dūnhuáng 敦煌. Around this time, the trade routes known as the Silk Roads (Sīchóu zhī lù 丝绸之路) were established and connected the Chinese and Roman empires. China imported wool and linen fabrics, amber, wine, gold coins and bullion from the Romans. Under Wu Di the Han became one of the most powerful empires in the world. According to the census of 1 CE, roughly the midpoint between the Western and Eastern Han, the population numbered about 60 million. Most were peasants who paid the government land and poll taxes; rendered corvée, and served in the army.

After Wu Di's reign came a cycle of governance that would recur often in Chinese history: a strong, effective ruler followed by ones who were young and weak. Regents, eunuchs, and the families of the emperors' consorts began to dominate court politics. In 9 CE, the regent Wáng Mǎng 王莽 (45 BCE–23 CE) claimed to have received the new Mandate of Heaven (divine justification for taking the throne). He seized imperial power and named his dynasty the Xīn 新 (New), but when attempts at reform failed his regime was overthrown by a large peasant rebellion. In 25 CE, Guāng Wǔdì 光武帝

Trade routes known as the Silk Roads connected the Chinese and the Roman empires.

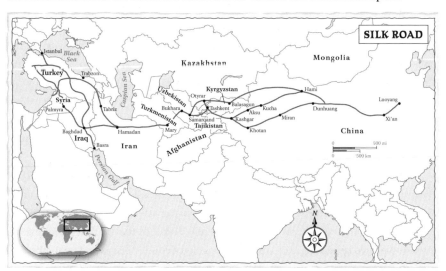

(6 BCE–57 CE), an educated Confucian scholar, won the support of other aristocratic clans and restored the Han house. The new dynasty, called the Eastern Han, established a network of great estates worked by tenant farmers and slaves, and moved its capital eastward from Chang'an to Luoyang. The Han became rich and strong again under Guang Wu Di's immediate successors.

After the reign of Hédì 和帝 (89–105 CE) the next ten Han emperors took the throne at ages between one hundred days and sixteen years. Powerful landowners evaded taxes and enlarged their holdings, trade declined, and cities shrank. The pendulum began to shift from centralization to decentralization.

Paper, Silk, and the Ingredients of Gunpowder (Zhǐ, sīchóu yǔ huǒyào de chéngfèn 纸、丝绸与火药的成分)

The most remarkable product of Han imagination was a composite paper (perhaps made from plant fibers, such as hemp and bark, and textile fibers, such as silk). Although the Chinese have long (and popularly) attributed this invention to Cài Lún 蔡伦 in the early second century CE, archaeologists in 1957 dated paper in China to 49 BCE; pure rag paper has been dated even earlier, to the second century BCE. The proliferation of paper—replacing other materials for writing, such as animal shells, oracle bones, and bamboo—made a significant contribution to the transmission of ideas and information in the premodern world. No doubt that the great Han historian Sima Qian, author of the first comprehensive history of China, *Shiji* (史记 *Records of the Grand Historian*), found it easier to write on paper than on bamboo strips: divided into five sections—basic annals, chronological tables, monographs, family chronologies, and biographies—this massive 116-chapter tome provided both historical information and moral instruction.

To enhance its economic development the Han sought to monopolize the production of iron, salt, silk, and copper in the early second century BCE. Silk was a valuable export, and bolts of the cloth were used as currency and given as state gifts. Craftspeople continued the Chinese tradition of excelling in metallurgy, and by the first century CE China had about fifty state-run ironworks. In the making of other crafts, wares, carvings, and sculpture, artisans turned increasingly to materials such as porcelain (a Chinese invention of the period), semiprecious stone, jade, lacquer, bronze, ceramic, and textiles.

Of course not all creativity was driven by economic necessity. Scholars interpret the interest in making ceramic spirit models, which depicted human figures in domestic settings, as a departure from mystical beliefs in the afterlife to a presumption that everyday activities would continue after death. Some of the literally monumental stone sculptures appearing by 100 BCE were erected in public places and on tombs that,

Cài Lún (蔡伦)

In *The 100: A Ranking of the Most Influential Persons in History*, Michael H. Hart placed Ts'ai Lun (also known as Cài Lún, c. 50–121 CE) as the seventh most influential figure in human history, edging out Johannes Gutenberg and Christopher Columbus, and coming in on the heels of Confucius and St. Paul. That's pretty good company for an obscure court eunuch from the Han dynasty. Cai Lun earned this distinction in 105 CE by presenting the emperor with a new invention: paper.

According to Hart, Western suspicions that Cai Lun is merely legendary can be dispelled by official Chinese histories. Han records mention that the emperor was pleased when Cai Lun gave him the gift, and understandably so. Transporting even a small number of bamboo record books required the use of a wheelbarrow. Storing them was unwieldy at best. Such logistics became more complicated when the imperial government expanded, and with it the amount of bureaucratic red tape. Cai Lun got a promotion and an aristocratic title. He got rich. He also got caught up in palace intrigue. Hart tells us that when Cai Lun was publicly disgraced, "he took a bath, dressed in his finest robes, and drank poison."

Paper was in common use in China by the third century CE, though it would be several more centuries before the technology made its way to the Arab world, and not until the twelfth century would knowledge of papermaking spread to Europe. Most books in the West before that time were written on parchment and vellum, materials made of specially (and expensively) processed sheepskin and calfskin; both had replaced the (also costly) papyrus and parchment used by Egyptians, Greeks, and Romans. Hart bases his ranking of Cai Lun above Gutenberg on three factors: (1) paper's cost-effectiveness and its versatility as a material for applications other than writing; (2) the possibility that Gutenberg would have never invented the movable-type printing press had paper not been invented; and (3) the assumption that if only one of the two had been invented, more books would have been block-printed on paper (a technique known by the Chinese as early as the seventh century) than produced by using movable type on parchment.

Hart credits paper, and by extension Cai Lun, as a key factor that allowed Chinese civilization to surpass the West: paper enabled a more rapid dissemination of knowledge and information than did parchment. But, Hart acknowledges, the West would soon narrow the gap when Gutenberg made possible the mass production of books.

Source: Michael H. Hart. (1978). *The 100: A Ranking of the Most Influential Persons in History*. New York: Kensington Publishing Group.

within another hundred years, would be filled with elaborate "burial goods" for use by imperial families and rich landowners.

Religious and intellectual life thus reflected dynamic changes. The first several Han emperors were led by the Daoist notion of "non-action" (*wúwéi* 无为), which emphasized frugal government and delegation of imperial authority. Historians attribute early Han prosperity partly to lenient government policies guided by Daoist ideas.

Emperor Wu Di, however, had desired a great empire, and non-action was hardly the most feasible way to achieve his goal. He embraced Confucianism, a belief system that advocated active social participation and adherence to traditional hierarchies. The great synthesizer of Confucian teachings of the time was Dǒng Zhòngshū 董仲舒 (c. 179–104 BCE), one of Wu Di's court advisers. According to Dong, if the human ruler received the Mandate of Heaven it was his duty to develop his subjects' moral goodness, help provide their livelihood, and maintain social and cosmic harmony.

During the Han, a new form of Daoism (called "religious Daoism") flourished. This trend was concerned primarily with the concoction of potions to prolong life and attain immortality, and with the use of alchemy to produce gold from base materials. Neither of these endeavors seems to have succeeded in its original goal, but both had some interesting side effects. One was the invention of the compass (based on the orienting effect that magnetite, or lodestone, had when placed on a nonconductive metal like bronze). Another was the discovery of sulfur and saltpeter, the ingredients of gunpowder. Although Daoist texts as early as 850 CE warned that mixing certain substances (including sulfur and saltpeter), could result in singed beards and blown-up houses, the earliest formula for gunpowder as we recognize it was not recorded until about 1000, and the first real gun did not appear until the thirteenth century.

The Legacy of the Han (Hàn cháo de yíchǎn 汉朝的遗产)

In 184 CE, as a response to political corruption and land annexation, peasant groups across north China known as the "Yellow Turbans" (Huángjīnjūn 黄巾军) revolted. Cáo Cāo 曹操 (155–220 CE) led the suppression of the rebels and then claimed the title of chancellor of the imperial government. In 220 CE, after Cao Cao died, his son Cáo Pī 曹丕 (reigned 220–226 CE as Wéndì 文帝 of the Wèi 魏 state) forced the last Han emperor to abdicate. China then entered a long period of disunity and disorder.

Topics for Further Study
Daoism—Religion
Han Rhapsodists
Silk
Southern and Northern Dynasties

Despite internal strife, the Han dynasty provided a model of a long-lasting, extensive, and unified empire. Its belief system, social structure, and economic form influenced later dynasties. The Han period, characterized for its technological progress and economic expansion, as well as for its classical expressions in courtly music, literature, and the dramatic and visual arts, gets less publicity in the West as a beacon of the ancient world than the Roman Empire, but Han achievements made China a dominant force in its time.

Southern and Northern Dynasties

Nán Běi cháo 南北朝
220–589 CE
(years debated by scholars)

After the decline and fall of the Roman Empire (a period considered by most scholars to have lasted about 320 years and to have ended in 476 CE), Europe went through centuries of fragmentation known as the Dark Ages. The period in China, from the end of the Han dynasty in 220 CE until the unification of the country by the Suí 隋 in 589 CE—during which no one dynasty ruled—in some ways mirrors that historical time.

This lack of unified rule spawns further debate among modern scholars who don't agree on the dates for the Southern and Northern Dynasties period. In fact, historians often disagree about whether the dynastic subgroups (factions or states) were official or unofficial, regional or local. (Some date a Three Kingdoms period [220–265 or 280 CE] as distinct from the Southern and Northern Dynasties, for instance, and mark the beginning of the Sui dynasty as 581 CE.) So this time in Chinese history, chaotic then, remains so now.

The name of the period, however, is logical. It refers to the internal strife between the north and the south after the fall of the Han, the migration of northern Chinese to southern China, and the movement of non-Chinese tribal peoples to the north. Four Southern dynasties preceded the five Northern dynasties, the latter including the Northern Zhou, from which came a general who would play a role in the founding of the Sui dynasty to follow.

The need to sort out the historical record might have seemed less than urgent, at least perhaps over time for the Chinese, because of the profound and far-reaching effect of the *Romance of the Three Kingdoms,* one of China's "Four Classic Novels." This long saga, attributed to Luó Guànzhōng 罗贯中 and dated somewhere near the end of the Yuán 元 (1279–1368) and beginning of the Míng 明 (1386–1164) dynasties, was based on the efforts of historians, storytellers, and dramatists over the preceding five centuries to chronicle the rise and fall of three kingdoms—the Wei, the Shǔ 蜀, and the Wú 吴—during the years from 169 to 280 CE. The novel organizes a century's worth of battles and the schemes of warring states into a flowing epic drama whose vividly portrayed characters have become an indelible part of Chinese cultural history.

Coping with Chaos (Yīngduì zhànluàn 应对战乱)

During the Southern and Northern Dynasties, often considered China's own Dark Age, the entire Huang River valley became a vast battlefield for tribal kingdoms. It was a time of great upheaval, and as a result the Chinese people became receptive as never before to Buddhism, the religion that had reached China from India (via the Silk Roads) in the middle of the first century CE. Han imperial rule had advocated Confucian ideals with their emphasis on family values, filial piety, social responsibility, and loyalty, none of which conformed to the Buddhist principles of monasticism, celibacy, and withdrawal from society. Daoism, however, not yet a formal religion, had become popular with the Chinese; its ideals focused on maintaining good health, increasing longevity, and achieving immortality, often through meditation. Buddhist texts, many on meditative practices, began to be translated from Sanskrit into Chinese. A technique called *géyì* 格义 (matching the meaning) involved the teaching and translating of a concept of Buddhism that had a similar Daoist counterpart: The word *dao* (way) was used to translate Buddhism's *dharma* (divine law). The alliance between the two traditions allowed Buddhism to gain a stronghold in China, especially as Buddhist practices offered consolation to a populace in turmoil after the fall of the Han. Eventually Buddhism became very influential in China, and the religion was adapted to indigenous Chinese culture and society. This trend continued for several centuries even after the country was reunited again in 589 CE.

Cultural Advances
(Wénhuà jìnbù 文化进步)

Despite political strife, important advances in

Topics for Further Study
Buddhism
Calligraphy
Poetry
Romance of Three Kingdoms

astronomy, mapmaking, medicine, and mathematics occurred in China during these "Dark Ages." Knowledge and the application of the sciences were held in high regard. Zǔ Chōngzhī 祖冲之 (429–500 CE), for example, an astronomer and mathematician, was esteemed in the south at the capital of Nánjīng for calculating the length of the solar year, predicting eclipses, and determining the value of pi.

Emperors of the south encouraged the recitation and writing of poetry, as well as calligraphy, painting, and musical composition. Imperial courts from the Sui dynasty on would employ professional painters, artisans, architects, and gardeners to shape the aesthetics of court life, but the practice had its roots in this period. The British Museum houses a famous work by one court painter, Gù Kǎizhī 顾恺之 (c. 344–406 CE): *Admonitions of the Court Instructress to Palace Ladies* (handscroll, ink and color on silk) conveyed strong Confucian moralistic messages about the ways in which women should conduct themselves (and thus exemplified the didactic qualities of art valued by Confucians). One of China's most revered calligraphers, Wáng Xīzhī 王羲之 (303?–379? CE) produced a work of such exquisite beauty—using brushstroke techniques described as "Leaning Dragon and Leaping Tiger" (龙卧虎跳 lóng-wò-hǔ-tiào)—that it became a treasure to connoisseurs and collectors of the Táng dynasty (618–907 CE). Emperor Tàizōng 太宗 (reigned 626–649 CE) found it so irresistible that he ordered it to be buried with him in his tomb.

Sui Dynasty: China United

Suí cháo: Zhōngguó tǒngyī

隋: 中国的统一

581–618 CE

*L*ike the Qin dynasty eight centuries earlier, the Sui dynasty united China and developed institutions that would influence the country for centuries to come. Also like the Qin, an emperor's harsh policies and the use of forced labor to achieve his oversized dreams resulted in a revolt that toppled the dynasty after less than forty years. Military campaigns thus characterize the period, but so do remarkable feats of engineering, the construction of great cities and palaces, legal and administrative reforms, and the assembly of a great library to house records that would establish the dynasty's cultural heritage. At the Sui empire's peak in 609 CE, it stretched about 5,022 kilometers (3,121 miles) east from the steppes of Tibet to the sea and 8,000 kilometers (4,971 miles) south from the Great Wall to Vietnam; its population reached just about 49 million people, the largest since the Han.

In 580, Yáng Jiān 杨坚 (541–604 CE), a general of the Northern Zhou dynasty, was appointed the regent for his grandson, the Zhou's new eight-year-old emperor (the boy was the son of Yang's eldest daughter and the Zhou emperor Xuāndì 宣帝, who had just died). Within a year, Yang Jian and his supporters had ruthlessly overthrown the imperial family, having sixteen of its princes and forty-one of their sons and brothers killed. Yang Jian named himself Wendi ("emperor of culture") of the new Sui dynasty, which controlled most of China north of the Yangzi River, a formidable barrier to traveling in or invading the south. Wendi claimed to be the legitimate heir of the great Han dynasty and set out to create as great an empire for himself. From 581 to 583 CE, he oversaw construction of a new capital city, Dàxīng 大兴, which was located about 10 kilometers (a little over 6 miles) from Chang'an (modern-day Xi'an). By 589 CE, after a series of military victories—a number of which were fought from a fleet of huge warships decked with five-story-high castles, each big enough to house eight hundred men—the Sui had reunified China.

Rapid Reforms (Léi-lì-fēng-xíng de gǎigé 雷厉风行的改革)

Sui Wendi introduced a state examination system, known as *kējǔ* 科举, aimed at recruiting talented commoners into the administration. He also reformed China's military. In the sixth century a system called *fǔbīng* 府兵 (garrison soldier) had been created in north China. In frontier regions threatened by nomads, garrisons were founded under the control of a dozen generals each. The families that provided soldiers to these garrisons were mostly non-Han Chinese minorities who were exempted from taxation and forced labor obligations. In 590, Wendi, a former *fǔbīng* general himself, declared that all military households be administered by local prefectures and counties. This brought the military under the control of civil officials. As a byproduct, the reform helped to integrate non-Han minorities into Chinese society—the segregation of minorities from the Han would be a frequent problem throughout China's history.

In 582 CE Wendi redefined the equal-field system (*jūntiánzhì* 均田制) for agriculture so that at age twenty-one a man was entitled to eighty *mu* (about 13 acres) of cultivated land from the state. A woman received half that amount. Peasants could pass the land to their children and had the freedom to sell it. In return, a peasant family had to pay rent, fulfill twenty days of conscripted labor a year, and give the state two bolts of cotton or silk cloth. This new policy succeeded in raising production of grain and cloth to historically high levels.

Although Wendi was sometimes cruel and hotheaded, his law, the Kāihuáng Code (开皇之治 Emperor's New Law) eliminated many cruel punishments, and officials who committed crimes could pay the fines from their salaries or accept official demotion. All in all, however, the changes Wendi instigated during his reign made China comparatively a more productive, prosperous, and less chaotic place.

Great Ambitions at a Great Price (Xióngxīn bóbó, dàijià chénzhòng 雄心勃勃, 代价沉重)

At Wendi's death in 604 CE, his second son, Yáng Guǎng 杨广 succeeded to the throne and declared himself Yángdì 炀帝 ("emperor of flaming"). His fourteen-year reign was marked by great successes but also by great failures, most notably his invasions of the kingdom of Koguryo (in modern Korea): of a million men sent on those campaigns, only 2,700 returned.

In 605 CE, with millions of conscripted laborers and at great cost, Yangdi began to build a second Sui capital in Luoyang, to the east of Chang'an, as well to add to the Grand Canal system that remained China's main mode of north–south transportation until the railroad in the nineteenth century. The first branch replaced an older canal linking the Huang (Yellow) River to the Yangzi; the second, extending from the Huang to a location near modern Beijing, which required conscripting women laborers as well as men, was intended to facilitate the transport of provisions to troops fighting in his Koguryo campaign; and the third, another replaced and repaired section, linked the Yangzi to Hangzhou—all for a total of about 2,357 kilometers (1,465 miles). No doubt the Grand Canal made it easier for the revenue from trade to be sent to the central government in the capitals, but it also provided an impressive waterway along which Yangdi traveled to and from his palace at Jiāngdū 江都—his ostentatious imperial flotilla comprised about 5,235 vessels and accommodated his entire court and its entourage.

One of Yangdi's legacies was to continue amassing manuscripts that would establish the cultural heritage of the dynasty, a project actually begun by Wendi in 583 CE. The library Yangdi commissioned in Luoyang to house these works was as notable for its "bells and whistles" as for its collection. When the emperor arrived, for instance, a maidservant carrying incense would lead him through the front hall where she would step on a mechanical device that triggered the rising of curtains and the swinging of doors. Inside were shelves laden with scrolls (89,666 of them, representing 14,466 titles, according to a catalogue compiled during the Tang dynasty, 618–907 CE).

Sparked by the constant demands for labor on such grand projects, peasant rebellions grew throughout north and central China. Yangdi lived luxuriously and avoided hearing bad news, so he knew little about how much he was resented. His officials lied to him—understandably, as one of them who spoke the truth was beaten to death for it. Eventually, some high-ranking officials organized a rebellion, and in 618 CE Yangdi was murdered in his bathhouse by a general. The Sui dynasty ended with him.

Tang Dynasty: Poetry and Literature

Táng cháo: shīgē yǔ wénxué
唐朝: 诗歌与文学
618–907 CE

The Tang dynasty (618–907 CE) marked the golden age of imperial China—a period in which the arts flourished, money drafts were invented, reforms were initiated that affected later dynasties, and cultural exchanges with neighboring countries like Japan, as well as with the West, were on the rise.

The dynasty's founder, Lǐ Yuān 李渊, had inherited the title "dynastic duke of Tang," and when the Sui collapsed he seized its capital and ascended to the throne in 618 CE. During the reign of Gāozǔ 高祖 (Li Yuan's reign name) from 618 to 626 CE, the Tang expanded and consolidated the empire. Gaozu revived the civil service exams to recruit government officials based on merit, not aristocracy, and he established mints and a new form of currency that remained standard throughout the dynasty's 297 years. Under his reign the Tang legal system, consisting of four components (the Code, Statutes, Regulations, and Ordinances), established a foundation for future imperial dynasties and later influenced the legal systems of Japan, Korea, and Vietnam. Gaozu's second son, Lǐ Shìmín 李世民 (reign name Tàizōng 太宗), seized the throne from his father in a military coup. His reign, from 626 to 649 CE, traditionally known as the "era of good government" (zhēnguān zhī zhì 贞观之治), was one of close personal interaction between the ruler and his Confucian advisers. Taizong also subdued the eastern Turks and began to expand Chinese power in central Asia.

Taizong's ninth son became Emperor Gāozōng 高宗, who reigned from 649 to 683 CE. His court came to be dominated by one of the most remarkable women in Chinese history, Wǔ Zétiān 武则天 (627–710 CE). Once a concubine of Taizong, she managed to become Gaozong's legitimate empress, take over the central government after he suffered a fatal stroke in 683 CE, and briefly interrupt Tang rule until 705 CE. (See the sidebar about her life and reign.)

After a series of political intrigues an emperor named Xuánzōng 玄宗 (reigned 712–756 CE) took the throne; the early years of his rule, marked by institutional

Empress Wu Zetian 武则天

The history of the emperors of China includes more than four thousand years and exactly one woman. Though Chinese empresses and regents have held great influence (see the later profile of Empress Dowager Cixi, for example), Wu Zetian (625–705 CE) was the only woman to rule China as an emperor in her own name.

At age thirteen, Wu Zetian entered the Chinese imperial court as a lowly ranked concubine to Emperor Taizong (reigned 626–649) of the Tang dynasty. When he died she became concubine and later empress to her stepson, Emperor Gaozong (reigned 650–683). When Gaozong died, Wu deposed her sons, declared herself emperor, and attempted to found her own dynasty. Wu began removing the entrenched aristocrats from the court and gradually expanded the civil service examination to recruit more men of merit to serve in the government. Her reign saw a stable economy, moderate taxation for the peasantry, and a healthy growth in the population; by the end of her reign, her empire included 60 million people.

Wu Zetian was a decisive, capable ruler in many ways. But later historians have been hostile to her, describing her as a despotic usurper of the emperor's throne. As a woman ruler, she did challenge the traditional patriarchal dominance found in China—but by any "ungendered" human standard, she was ruthless in her personal/political dealings, allegedly murdering two sons, a daughter, and other relatives who opposed her. In 705, she was forced to abdicate, and she died later that year. Her son Zhongzong was again enthroned, and the Tang dynasty was restored.

progress, economic prosperity, and cultural flowering, were the heyday of the Tang. Under Xuanzong the aristocracy began to reassert its dominance over those who had received official positions through examinations. But from the 740s on the emperor took little interest in government affairs, distracted as he was by the charms of his concubine Yáng Guìfēi 杨贵妃, one of the so-called Four Beauties in Chinese history. His close advisers struggled for power, while his prime minister abolished the *fubing* system—in which garrison soldiers farmed the land during the growing season and at other times served in the military at the capitals and on the frontiers—and replaced it with a professional army. Ān Lùshān 安禄山, one of these career soldiers whose ancestors came from modern-day Uzbekistan, became an advisor to Xuanzong and eventually betrayed him by leading a rebellion that nearly destroyed the dynasty. The uprising lasted from 755 to 763 CE (although An Lushan himself was assassinated in 757); some 150,000 to 200,000 multiethnic rebel troops seized the Tang capitals of Luoyang and Chang'an, and controlled most of north China. Xuanzong fled to Sichuan Province.

After the rebellion was put down the Tang lost its grip on many frontier areas; Tibetans saw the chance to infiltrate the western provinces of Gansu and Níngxià, for example, when the Tang withdrew to defend the capital. The authority of the central government declined, and some northern regions became virtually autonomous. At the same time eunuch court officials began to play an increasing role in Tang politics. Although Xiànzōng 宪宗, the emperor who reigned from 805 to 820 CE, had managed to stifle rebellions in Sichuan and put the Tang back in control of several powerful provinces, the credit belonged to loyal eunuchs who controlled palace armies and administration of the provinces. Xianzong's eunuchs eventually murdered him, however, and for the most part determined the succession of young emperors during the remaining years of the dynasty.

In the course of its last several decades, the Tang dynasty suffered from serious floods and droughts as well as political chaos and foreign threats. In 874 CE, a wave of peasant rebellions broke out. During one uprising led by Huáng Cháo 黄巢, a failed civil service examinee turned salt smuggler, starving peasants and criminal gangs sacked Guǎngzhōu (Canton), where thousands of resident Islamic traders were massacred. The rebel forces were finally suppressed, but the dynasty was rendered powerless. Most of the empire was occupied by non-Chinese forces or controlled by rival military leaders. In 907 CE, the warlord Zhū Wēn 朱温 ended the Tang and established his own Liáng 梁 dynasty at the beginning of the Five Dynasties period (907–960 CE).

Society and Culture (Shèhuì yǔ wénhuà 社会与文化)

The Tang was a cosmopolitan society open to foreign influence. About two million people lived in the capital Chang'an, making it the most populous city in the world. Foreign goods were displayed in the marketplaces of the major cities, and some foreign customs, such as playing polo, became fashionable. Foreign students went to China to study the Tang's religions, culture, and political achievements. The Japanese, for example, learned much from the Tang about Confucianism, Buddhism, literature, art, architecture, bureaucracy, and codes of law.

After the An Lushan rebellion the equal-field land distribution system collapsed, changing the social hierarchy and structure to some extent. Many peasants gave up ownership of their lands and, on a contractual basis, became tenants or laborers; rich,

Polo players in the heat of the game, a pastime introduced to China from Persia, appear in this detail from a Tang-era tomb painting, part of the larger Qianling Mausoleum near Xi'an (formerly Chang'an, the Tang capital).

local elites seized the opportunity to establish large, landed estates managed by bailiffs and cultivated by workers, tenants, or slaves. Thus a new ruling class obtained political power from education and ownership of land rather than from aristocratic birth. After the mid-750s, the old taxation system ceased to function. During Dézōng's 德宗 reign (779–805 CE), a new system combined various levies into a single tax to be paid in the summer and autumn. It was based on the value of property instead of number of household members and remained China's basic tax structure until the sixteenth century.

The rise of Buddhism in China continued under the Tang, even though the court endorsed Daoism, claiming that Li Yuan (Emperor Gaozu) was a descendant of Daoism's alleged founder, Laozi. For most of the period the Tang recognized the strength of Buddhism and provided it with patronage. The efforts of a Chinese-born Buddhist monk named Xuánzàng 玄奘 (602?–664 CE)—who made a pilgrimage to India, returned sixteen years later with hundreds of Buddhist scriptures (sutras), and spent the rest of his life translating them with linguists and Buddhist scholars—contributed significantly to the Chinese understanding of Indian Buddhist doctrines

Journey to the West: On the Road with Xuanzang

No doubt the real-life journey of the Chinese Buddhist monk Xuanzang was quite an adventure. Setting out to India in search of Buddhist sutras (scriptures), he crossed the war-torn border of Chang'an and made his way northwest toward the Tian Shan range. He followed the southern edge of the mountains some 2,400 kilometers (about 1490 miles) to Turpan, a city in the Tarim Basin. He then passed through modern-day Kyrgyzstan, Tajikistan, Afghanistan, and Pakistan. Once in Gandhara he made a circuitous route through the Indian subcontinent before heading home.

But it's highly unlikely that his traveling companions were as exotic as the pilgrim band escorting the fictional Xuanzang in *Xiyou ji* (*Journey to the West*), a novel believed to written or compiled by Wú Chéng'ēn 吴承恩 in the sixteenth century. The book, which combines allegory, gentle satire, humor, and lots of magical realism, draws on Daoist, Buddhist, and Confucian thought. It is still a rich source for adaptation in storytelling, opera, theater, puppetry, comic books, television, and video games, both in China and abroad.

The cast of characters includes exotic and four powerful creatures assigned to protect Xuanzang on his journey: Monkey, who carries with him a pair of walking shoes made from lotus roots, a phoenix-winged purple and gold helmet, a suit of golden chain mail, and three live-saving magic hairs; Pigsy, once the immortal officer of troops in the Milky Way, who was banished to Earth for getting drunk and flirting with the Moon Princess; Sandy, the river monster that Pigsy and Monkey subdue (he turns out to be the most polite and obedient of the disciples); and Third Prince of the Dragon King, who turns into a white horse Xuanzang can ride to escape from danger.

Lots of struggles ensue, almost to the last (one-hundredth chapter), which is set in a wilderness with flaming mountains, impossibly wide rivers, and numerous monsters. In the end the monk gets the scriptures he came for and the characters receive their rewards: the monk and Monkey become Buddhas, Pigsy is named an altar cleanser, Sandy becomes an *arhat* (spiritual practitioner), and the white horse becomes a heavenly dragon.

and philosophies. (See the sidebar about *Journey to the West*, a novel based in part on Xuanzang's travels.)

From 843 to 845 CE, however, the pro-Daoist emperor Wǔzōng 武宗 persecuted Buddhists, and some 4,600 monasteries and 40,000 shrines and temples were destroyed. This was the beginning of Buddhism's decline in China. The Daoist backlash against Buddhism had its roots in the increasing incursions by non-Chinese ethnicities and, in some ways, the Tang's cosmopolitan openness. Buddhism, despite its growing stronghold in China over five centuries, began to be seen by native reactionaries as "foreign." Buddhism thus was attacked for subverting Chinese family values and the sociopolitical hierarchy at the heart of Confucian philosophy. Attitudes to Buddhism had come full circle.

For more than three thousand years, poetry has been deemed the pinnacle of literary achievement in China, and during the Tang period poetry undoubtedly reached its peak. Lǐ Bái 李白 (701–762 CE) and Dù Fǔ 杜甫 (712–770 CE) are among the most acclaimed poets. Although Li Bai's talents were not fully recognized by the Tang court—and even today he is stereotypically associated with poems about drinking too much wine—Li's poetry can be characterized by his strong passion, his use of powerful rhetorical devices, and the innovative changes he made to traditional verse forms. Many of Du Fu's poems explore people's suffering in times of war and famine, such as "The Old Man With No Family to Take Leave Of" (*Shíháolì* 石壕吏).

A Poem by Li Bai

I Hike Up Dai Tian Mountain, But the Daoist Is Not at Home

I can hear a stream and a barking dog
and the smell of dewy peach flowers hangs in the morning air.
Through the deep trees I get glimpses of deer.
The noon bell is drowned by the sounds of water.
Mist rises between the wild bamboo and the green mountain.
Thin waterfalls hang in the air before the looming peak.
No one knows where he went.
I lean against two close pines and feel the sadness.

Translated by Donald Junkins

Modern-day Westerners needing a reminder about the lasting influence of Tang achievements take note: today the character that refers literally to the Tang as a dynasty (唐) is often translated synonymously as "Chinese" or "China." For instance, traditional Chinese jackets, which garnered renewed popularity after world leaders were photographed wearing them at the 2001 APEC (Asia-Pacific Economic Cooperation) summit in China, are called *tángzhuāng* 唐装, meaning "Tang-style clothing," even though they were modeled on a design from the late Qing dynasty (1644–1911/12). And Chinese emigrants refer to their communities in foreign countries (Chinatowns) as *tángrénjiē* 唐人街—the "streets of the Tang people."

Five Dynasties and Ten Kingdoms

Wǔ dai Shi guó 五代十国
907–960 CE

*T*he Five Dynasties and Ten Kingdoms (五代十国 *Wudai shiguo*)—or Ten Nations—was a tumultuous period of Chinese history named for the five successive short-lived dynasties (none reigned more than sixteen years) and the ten major kingdoms that existed from the fall of the Tang dynasty in 907 CE to the succession of the Song dynasty in 960 CE.

In northern China, dynasties succeeded each other in rapid succession, while in southern China polities (headed by regional military governors called *jiédùshǐ* 节度使) existed concurrently, each controlling a specific geographical area. During years plagued by anarchy, corruption, and social upheaval in northern China its irrigation system failed and severe damage ensued: canals silted and dams fell into disrepair, floods devastated the countryside, and famine was widespread. The nearly continuous warfare in chaotic northern China led to the displacement of peasant farmers and village craftsmen who became refugees and fled to southern China.

In the south a still-stable society was able to facilitate the development of technology, science, culture, and the arts. Painters, calligraphers, and poets emerged from the south during this period, notably Lǐ Yǔ 李煜, renowned as a great master of the *cí* 词 (song lyric) poems in Chinese literary history. In 910 the king of the Wú Yuè 吴越 state built the Hanhaitang Dike in present-day Zhejiang Province to facilitate agricultural production and (not coincidentally) to enhance his own wealth and position. The Chǔ 楚 kingdom made significant technological advances in the manufacturing of porcelain and the development of printing; the latter resulted in the publication of the first complete set of 130 volumes of Confucian writings as well as numerous Buddhist and Daoist classics.

Nonetheless, southern China also suffered from endemic warfare as the Wu Yue fought with other polities until they were supplanted by the Southern Tang. Political and administrative crises among other groups gave the Southern Tang the opportunity to strengthen its position, and although for a while it became the most powerful polity in southern China, it was unable to repel the incursions by other warring states. The Northern Sòng 北宋 dynasty, established in 960 CE, sought to reunify China and by 978 CE had brought all of southern China under the control of the central government.

Song Dynasty

Sòng cháo 宋朝 960–1279:
Northern Song (960–1126);
Southern Song (1127–1279)

The Song dynasty 宋 (960–1279) defined a new and enduring phase of China's premodern civilization, including the shift of the economy to the south, the flourishing of urban culture, a revival of the classical heritage in the attempt to displace Buddhism, and a new class of civil administrators trained to serve the imperial autocracy. The Song is divided into two periods: the Northern Song (960–1126) ended when its capital city, Kāifēng 开封, in north China, was captured by the Jurchen Jīn (Nüzhēn Jīn cháo 女真金朝) dynasty. The Southern Song

南宋 continued until Mongols captured its capital Lín'ān 临安 (now Hángzhōu), south of the Yangzi River, and began the Yuan 元 dynasty in 1279.

Northern Song (Běi Sòng 北宋)

In 960 CE, Zhào Kuāngyìn 赵匡胤, the commander-in-chief of the palace army of the Later Zhou dynasty 后周 (a part of the Five Dynasties and Ten Kingdoms period, 907–960 CE) feared invasion from the northeast by a feudal tribe called the Khitan 契丹; he led a mutiny to claim the imperial throne from the reigning child emperor and founded the Song dynasty. Zhao's belief, that the urgent need for competent rule justified his disloyalty to the immature sovereign, was an ethical conundrum faced by many imperial dynasties, and historians have generally sanctioned Zhao's decision. Aware that the same thinking could provoke the overthrow of his own throne, Zhao persuaded his commanders to accept a lavish retirement package and "work" under his close scrutiny; he thus established a centralized military power that remained characteristic for much of Song rule. As Emperor Tàizǔ, Zhao stressed the Confucian spirit of humane administration and enhanced the prestige of government recruitment through the civil service examinations. Candidates for office had to memorize the Confucian classics and answer rigorous questions regarding statecraft and imperial policies. The dynasty focused on threats from non-Chinese states primarily in the northeast near modern Beijing, and established a capital in Kaifeng located in eastern Henan Province.

Before the mid-Tang period, China's few large cities existed primarily to facilitate government administration and taxation, conscription of the peasant population as laborers, and regional military control. Private commerce was relatively undeveloped, and state monopolies were in charge of producing strategic goods essential to

Thought Experiment

Why were Confucian ideals—and civil service examinations that required candidates for office to memorize Confucian classics—so important to rulers like Emperor Taizu? Why was it so important for him to foster a "spirit of humane administration" in government officials? Do you see similarities or differences in the way U.S. politicians used the concept of "family values" to gain political favor in the first years of the twenty-first century?

maintaining a balanced peasant economy—salt and tools for ironworking and luxuries like silks, some of which were exported overland to western Asia at great profit. In early imperial capitals such as Chang'an residents typically lived in closed courtyards, and night curfews were enforced. When Kaifeng became the Song capital, it was already a well-developed commercial city with a flourishing economic and social life that continued unabated. A famous horizontal handscroll more than 5 meters (some 16.5 feet) long known as *Peace Reigns over the River* (Qīngmíng shànghétú 清明上河图) vividly portrays with realistic and colorful detail the elegance and raw human energy of daily life in and near the Northern Song capital.

Under Emperor Shénzōng's reign (1068–1085) his chief counselor Wáng Ānshí 王安石 instituted significant reforms that were precursors of the modern era. For example, about a millennium before such U.S. agencies as the Small Business Administration, Wang created a fund for low-interest agricultural loans to farmers and small merchants who could then avoid the exorbitant demands of moneylenders. Wang also ordered a new land survey to assess taxes more fairly and a village militia system for local policing. Large landowners, big merchants, and moneylenders, however, attacked the reformers and forced Wang to resign.

Failed reforms, along with the extravagance and corruption of the court of Emperor Huīzōng 徽宗 (1101–1125) weakened the Northern Song dynasty, while in the early twelfth century the Jin 金 dynasty of the Jurchen (Nǚzhēn 女真) nation, which would rule China as the Jurchen Jin dynasty from 1125 to 1234, rose to power northern Manchuria. The Jurchen Jin attacked the Song capital of Kaifeng in 1126, captured the Chinese emperor and his clan members, sent them to Manchuria, and ended the Northern Song.

Southern Song (Nán Sòng 南宋)

In 1127 Song loyalists put Gāozōng 高宗 (reigned 1127–1162) on the throne and established the Southern Song in Hangzhou. In 1141, while concluding peace negotiations with the Jurchen Jin dynasty, Gaozong ordered the execution of one of his generals, Yuè Fēi 岳飞 (1103–1141), who had criticized the emperor's willingness to bargain for peace. Yue Fei later became a symbol of patriotism for refusing to give up on restoring all of China's lost territory. In the treaty of 1142, the Song agreed to make annual payments to the Jin and recognized the Jin as its superior. The Jurchen Jin continued their raids of the Southern Song until they were destroyed by

Topics for Further Study
Banking—History
Foot-binding
Papermaking and Printing
Women, Role of

the combined attacks of the Mongols and the Southern Song in 1234. The Southern Song dynasty ended in 1279 when the last imperial heir died in Guangzhou.

Markets, Paper Money, and the Abacus (Shìchǎng, zhǐbì, suànpán 市场、纸币、算盘)

During the Song period, the economic focus of the dynasty shifted south to the rice-growing region of the Yangzi River where new types of rice produced two or three crops a year, and the increased yields were enough to sustain a population of more than 100 million. The Song also developed a market economy, and shops and stalls in cities and towns sold products drawn from all over the country. An early type of bank, called a deposit shop, was developed to facilitate transactions. Merchants used drafts called *fēiquàn* 飞券 ("flying money"), and in the eleventh century, the Song became the first rulers in the world to issue paper money, as paper itself was not yet widely known in Europe at the time.

In this period China had numerous cities with over a hundred thousand people, several approaching a million, and perhaps 2 million in the capital of Hangzhou. Women had the right to own and inherit property and legally remarry. Women such as the great poet Lǐ Qīngzhào 李清照 (1084–c. 1151) contributed to the cultural output of the dynasty. Song women did suffer a decline in social standing with the spread of foot binding, a custom that was not completely abandoned until the twentieth century.

Another development of the Song period was the advent of neo-Confucianism. During the Northern Song, a new Confucian metaphysics emerged, borrowing from Daoism, Buddhism, and classical Confucianism. Zhū Xī 朱熹 (1130–1200) later synthesized these ideas into a belief system that was labeled either "Learning of Principle" (*lǐxué* 理学) or "Learning of the Way" (*dàoxué* 道学). This school of thought was later declared the state orthodoxy and guided imperial dynasties until the early twentieth century.

In the arts and culture of the period, landscape painting flourished, and the Song style of lyric poetry and prose has had a long-lasting influence. Great literary projects were completed, including the *Tàipíng yùlǎn* 太平御览 (*Imperially Reviewed Encyclopedia of the Taiping Era*) and *Cèfǔ yuánguī* 册府元龟 (*Outstanding Models from the Storehouse of Literature*). Song scholars wrote books about bronze bells and coins from the Zhou era and thus began scientific archaeology in China—in other words, people of the eleventh and twelfth century looked to uncover what was to *them* ancient history. The most famous Song historical work was the *Zī zhì tōngjiàn* 资治通鉴 (*Comprehensive Mirror for Aid in Government*) by Sīmǎ Guāng 司马光 (1019–1086). It told the history of China from 403 BCE to 959 CE. Another historical work, from around 1170, was called *Tōngjiàn jìshì běnmò* 通鉴纪事本末 (*Comprehensive Mirror, Topically Arranged*).

By the middle of the eleventh century an artisan named Bì Shēng 毕升 had invented movable characters for printing, three centuries before the German inventor Johannes Gutenberg. Since Chinese printing was done by carved woodblock techniques, his invention didn't really take hold. The components of explosive powder had been discovered during the Han dynasty (206 BCE–220 CE), but it was during the Song that the material we know as gunpowder today was applied in various grenades, bombs, and rocket launchers. In a quieter development, the abacus was invented, enabling people to calculate easily the many developments from this era of Chinese history.

Jurchen Jin Dynasty

Nü zhēn Jīn cháo 女真金朝
1125–1234

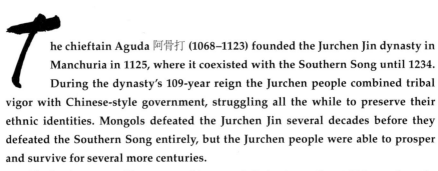

The chieftain Aguda 阿骨打 (1068–1123) founded the Jurchen Jin dynasty in Manchuria in 1125, where it coexisted with the Southern Song until 1234. During the dynasty's 109-year reign the Jurchen people combined tribal vigor with Chinese-style government, struggling all the while to preserve their ethnic identities. Mongols defeated the Jurchen Jin several decades before they defeated the Southern Song entirely, but the Jurchen people were able to prosper and survive for several more centuries.

The Jurchen were a Tungus-speaking people living in northeast China and southeastern Siberia. In the eleventh century there were two groups of Jurchen—one a group of tribesmen living the traditional life isolated in the north, the other a group that had interacted with the Khitan, the rulers of the Liáo 辽 dynasty (906–1125) in north China, and with the many Chinese ruled by the Khitan.

Aguda, founder of the Jurchen state, learned from the Khitan how to use cavalry effectively in warfare. After a series of raids along Liao's western frontiers, Aguda began taking the Liao subordinate capitals one by one, sometimes with the help of the

Northern Song. Aguda's successor Wú Qǐmǎi 吴乞买, or Taizong (1075–1135), began a massive invasion of the Song, his former ally. After the Northern Song collapsed, the entire north came under Jin control. China was divided between two equally powerful regimes, the Jurchen Jin and the Southern Song, with a third regime, the Xī Xià 西夏 state, occupying the northwest.

Struggles with the Song continued, and the Jin elite fought among themselves about how much Chinese influence they should absorb in their dynasty. The conflict, still unresolved when the Mongols invaded, was one reason why the Mongols conquered the Jin with relative ease—in part by allying themselves with the same tribes that the Jurchen people had befriended during their own rise.

Yuan Dynasty: Mongol Rule

Yuán cháo: Mónggǔrén de tǒngzhì
元朝: 蒙古人的统治
1279–1368

The Mongols, nomadic invaders from central Asia, conquered China in the late thirteenth century under the leadership of Khubilai Khan 忽必烈汗 (1215–1294), the grandson of Chinggis (Genghis) Khan 成吉思汗. During their rule as the Yuan 元 dynasty the Mongols borrowed extensively from other traditions, creating a uniquely multi-ethnic political and cultural environment. (Mongols ruled over several domains [khanates] in Eurasia at the time—the Il-Khan dynasty in Persia, the Golden Horde in Russia, and the Chagatai in central Asia, each a separate geopolitical unit diplomatically connected by trade.) While many aspects of Mongolian rule over China vanished with the dynasty in 1368, some political, military, and social features survived to influence China's last two dynasties, the Ming (1368–1644) and the Qing (1644–1911/12).

Chinggis (Genghis) Khan 成吉思汗

Chinggis Khan (a title meaning "resolute leader") was born circa 1162 with the name Temujin 铁木真. (He is popularly known in the West as Genghis Khan.) In 1185, after surviving tribal wars in Mongolia and the death of his father, the young Temujin built his own steppe confederation and rose to power. With power came numerous setbacks and hard-won victories. Among these was the kidnapping of his wife, Borte, by the Merkit tribe. Although Temujin eventually freed her from her captors, almost a year had passed and Borte was pregnant. Temujin accepted Jochi (d. 1225), as the child was named, but scholars have little doubt that he was the son a Merkit man. (Jochi's ancestry later became an issue in determining a successor for Temujin.)

Mongols supported Temjin over other steppe leaders because he was a charismatic social revolutionary. Rather than favor the aristocracy, he implemented laws that made tribal life more egalitarian—by divvying up the plunder from battles more equitably, for instance. By 1206, Temujin, now called by his new title, Chinggis Khan, was the dominant power in Mongolia. He went on to conquer much of northern China and central Asia. Motivated as often by retaliation as by greed for territory or riches, his strategic and organizational genius created one of the most highly disciplined and effective armies in history. *Mongol*, an Academy Award–winning, three-part epic made in 2007, depicts with gritty detail, including a scene about the kidnapping of Borte, the adventurous life of this most feared and respected leader.

Chinggis Khan died from injuries sustained after falling from a horse during a hunting expedition in 1227. His grandson Khubilai Khan, after years of struggling for power with his brothers, became the ruler of the China's Yuan dynasty in 1279.

Khubilai Khan helped win Chinese acceptance of foreign rule by giving his dynasty a Chinese name and welcoming several prominent Chinese scholars as advisors; he established his court and the Yuan capital in Dàdū 大都 (modern Beijing) to keep the symbolic center of rule in China. Western and central Asians such as Turks, Uygurs, Persians, and Tibetans, however, held high-level positions in the Yuan bureaucracy. Tensions built between ethnic factions at court and Chinese who felt that foreigners cared little about traditional Confucian values. Some Chinese saw Tibetans as arrogantly interfering with the administration of justice and claiming privileged status for themselves; some characterized Muslim financial advisors as usurers and embezzlers for imposing too severe a tax burden on the Chinese people. Nevertheless, the Mongols united China once again, and the Chinese believed that by doing so the Yuan had won the Mandate of Heaven (the divine right to rule). One remarkable aspect of the Yuan dynasty was its openness to all religions. Clergy of any tradition were untaxed; and churches, temples, and mosques were left alone as long as they didn't oppose Mongolian rule.

Artistic Expression and Rampant Inflation (Yìshù biǎoxiàn yǔ tōnghuò péngzhàng 艺术表现与通货膨胀)

Because they were blocked from government service as scholar-officials, many educated Chinese turned to the arts. Popular drama grew as a genre, and at least 160 Yuan-era plays called *zájù* 杂剧—song dramas that alternated arias with spoken dialogue, and which often exposed social problems of the era—are still known. The Yuan also produced many great Chinese painters; because the dynasty rarely scrutinized or censored thematic content or style, artists such as Zhào Mèngfǔ 赵孟頫 (1254–1322), who served the court in an official capacity (also as a poet, musician, and calligrapher), were free to experiment with different genres and techniques.

Trade and communication grew throughout the empire. Government postal stations enabled authorized officials and merchants to travel great distances quickly with fresh horses supplied at each of the more than 1,400 stations. Using some 3 million

Zhao Mengfu, in *Horse and Groom in the Wind* (ink on paper), used delicate brushstrokes to convey the power of the wind.

conscripted laborers, Khubilai Khan extended the Grand Canal so that grain from the Yangzi River region could be shipped north to the capital. Paper currency was used more widely than ever before. The Yuan court couldn't resist the temptation to print more money when revenues were needed for military campaigns or to make up for fiscal mismanagement. Inflation was one factor contributing to the collapse of the dynasty in 1368.

Military defeats were another factor. During Khubilai's reign, the Mongols successfully conquered Korea, but their naval attacks on Japan in 1274 and 1281 failed. Military expeditions into Southeast Asia in the 1270s and 1280s also met stiff resistance. Khubilai's successors abandoned further expansionism, and the dynasty fell into decline. Widespread popular revolts rose in the 1350s and 1360s, along with a series of major floods, droughts, and epidemics. The once fearsome Mongols fled and returned to Mongolia in 1368, getting out before the arrival of a rebel leader named Zhū Yuánzhāng 朱元璋.

Ming Dynasty: Building the Great Wall

Míng cháo: Chángchéng jiànshè
明朝: 长城建设
1368–1644

Zhu Yuanzhang was the only commoner, besides Gaozu, founder of the Han dynasty in 206 BCE, to hold the title "Emperor of China." As the son of a farmer, Zhu had been driven by extreme poverty to become a Buddhist monk, and during the chaos of the last Yuan decades the Mongols destroyed his monastery. Eager for revenge, Zhu rose to rebel-leader status when his forces competed with other warlord groups against the Yuan. In 1356, he conquered an important Yuan stronghold, Nánjīng 南京, one of the major urban centers in the region. He renamed the city Yìngtiānfǔ, 应天府 ("Capital Responsive to Heaven"), barely couching his imperial ambitions in the Mandate of Heaven by then so ingrained in Chinese dynastic history. **Months before Zhu's generals ousted Mongol forces from the capital Dadu in 1368, he prematurely announced the establishment of a new dynasty, the Ming (meaning "brilliance" or "illumination").**

After years of Mongol rule in the Yuan dynasty, the Ming gradually became an era of Chinese cultural revival. Zhu, who chose the reign name "Hóngwǔ 洪武," meaning "Grand Martiality," sought to restore Confucian values. He ordered that Chinese customs replace Mongol practices in marriage, dress code, family relations, social hierarchy, and rituals. Hongwu took a particular interest in education and had government and private schools established throughout the empire. In 1370 he reestablished the civil service exams that the Yuan had abandoned, suspended them after disappointing results in 1373, and reinstated them once more in 1385. Frustrated and suspicious of his government officials, Hongwu launched frequent and vicious purges of the bureaucracy, the military, and the general populace, executing thousands in campaigns that destabilized and often paralyzed the young dynasty. Preoccupied with protecting Ming boundaries, driving back Mongol forces to the north, and subduing non-Han tribes in Yúnnán to the southwest, he built up the Ming army to include 1 million soldiers. In 1380 Hongwu charged his chancellor with treason, had him executed, abolished the position, and in effect became his own chief minister. (His autocratic nature in governing has been labeled "Ming despotism" by some historians.) Not long afterward, the emperor appointed a small group of scholars from the top echelon of the bureaucracy to advise him informally and ease the burden of his administrative responsibilities. From this group the formalized institution of the Grand Secretariat evolved. It remained at the top of the bureaucratic power structure for the rest of the imperial era.

After Hongwu's death in 1398, his twenty-two-year-old grandson, the Jiànwén 建文 emperor (reigned 1398–1402), took the throne, but civil war broke out in 1399 when Zhū Dì 朱棣, the Prince of Yān 燕 (one of Hongwu's sons), attacked the imperial forces. Much of the countryside, which had barely recovered from the violence of the dynastic transition, was devastated. The prince and his troops captured Nanjing, and the palace burned to the ground during the battle. The Jianwen emperor died in the flames— although legend has it that he miraculously escaped—and Zhu Di ascended the throne.

Zhu Di, as the Yǒnglè 乐永 emperor (1360–1424, reigned 1402–1424), transferred the capital from Nanjing to Beijing in 1421. The city, called Dadu by the Yuan, became Běipíng 北平 (Northern Peace) when the Ming took over in 1368. Yongle, whose reign name means "Everlasting Happiness," finally renamed the capital Beijing (Northern Capital) after a fifteen-year-long reconstruction project during which thousands of

Zhèng Hé 郑和

Commercial maritime trade between China and other countries had been going on for several centuries before Admiral Zheng He (1371–1433) commanded six of the seven Ming expeditions that sailed from 1405 to 1433. These imperial-sponsored voyages were not made for trade or discovery—maps of the coasts of Asia and Africa had been drawn before the expeditions began—but for the chance to spread China's influence in foreign lands.

Zheng He was born to Muslim parents who named him Ma He ("Ma" was short for "Muhammad"). Although the Mongol ruled Yuan dynasty had tolerated his family's religion, with the rise of the Ming came religious persecution, and Ma He's family was killed. Ma He was castrated as a young boy—a practice conducted in many societies and cultures throughout history so that males, afterward called eunuchs, would be "suitable" to play certain social roles (ranging from court domestic, official, or advisor to choir singer or guardian of a harem)—and became an attendant in the Ming court. When the Yongle emperor came to power he heard Ma He repeat the seafaring stories his grandfather had told about traveling to Mecca for the hajj (pilgrimage); the emperor became intrigued with the possibility of expanding China's diplomatic horizons across the water. Eventually Yongle authorized the newly named Zheng He to oversee the construction of a fleet of "treasure ships" and plan a series of maritime missions.

The first of Zheng He's seven voyages included more than 27,800 men and 317 ships; his largest ships, by conservative estimates, were at least 122 meters (400 feet) long. (By comparison, the USS *Constitution*, built almost four hundred years later, was only half that size.) Zheng He's fleets sailed to the shores of the Indian Ocean, touching on the eastern coast of Africa and into the Red Sea. Wherever the ships appeared Zheng He collected rarities as gifts and demanded that local rulers recognize the dominion of China and the Yongle emperor.

The scale of Zheng He's expeditions dwarfed that of the Portuguese explorer Vasco da Gama, who would start on his voyage to India in 1497 with just four ships; but unlike the Portuguese discovery of the sea route to India, Zheng He's voyages had no lasting effect on China or the world. Although his naval expeditions won friends for the Ming, they did not bring in enough revenue to cover their extravagant cost. (Many historians believe that Zheng He and the Ming fleets had the capability to reach the Americas, had discovery been their priority.) After the death of Yongle, support for such expeditions died, and the imperial navy's fleet was left to rot. Thus the world lost its chance to see how things might have been different if the Chinese had reached the West Indies before Christopher Columbus.

laborers built new walls, palaces, gardens, streets, residential areas—and two of the modern city's most famous landmarks, Tiānānmén Gate 天安门 and Gùgōng 故宫 (the imperial palace known as the Forbidden City). A determined expansionist, Yongle ordered seven maritime expeditions to demand tribute from foreign rulers, chiefly under the command of Zhèng Hé 郑和 (1371–1433), a Muslim eunuch admiral. (See the sidebar about Admiral Zheng He.)

Defined Roles and a Growing Population (Rénhòu guǎnlǐ yǔ zēngzhǎng 人口管理与增长)

The Ming's founder, Hongwu, envisioned a simple way of life for his empire based on an agricultural economy. To restore a stable order after the chaos of the late Yuan, Hongwu established an array of social policies to regulate local society. The population of about 60 million was assigned to "hereditary households" and categorized, for example, as peasants, soldiers, artisans, and "mean people" (such as servants and prostitutes). Ming society was organized into communities called *lǐ jiǎ* 里甲, in which every 110 households formed a basic unit responsible for paying taxes, maintaining order, and promoting morality through mutual surveillance.

By the mid-sixteenth century, however, some industries expanded into major enterprises. In Jiāngxī Province, thousands of laborers worked in nearly thirty paper factories. Large textile workshops with more than 100,000 looms made Sōngjiāng 松江 (near Shanghai) a cotton-weaving center. At Jǐngdézhèn 景德镇, Jiangxi Province, a city with a population of 1 million, numerous porcelain kilns produced fine wares—some being the world-renowned Ming vases. New crops such as peanuts, corn, white potatoes, and sweet potatoes from the Americas helped lead to rapid population growth by expanding arable land into areas too hilly and too dry for more traditional crops. By the end of the dynasty, the Ming Empire included about 150 million people.

Arts and Scholarship (Yìshù yǔ xuéwèn 艺术与学问)

Popular culture flourished during the Ming. Long novels of the period included *Shuǐhǔ zhuàn* 水浒传 (*The Water Margin,* also called *All Men Are Brothers*, from the fourteenth century), *Sānguó yǎnyì* 三国演义 (*The Romance of the Three Kingdoms*, 1522), *Xīyóujì* 西游记 (*Journey to the West*, 1592), and *Jīn píng méi* 金瓶梅 (*The Golden Lotus*, 1617). Large short-story collections included *Pāi'àn jīngqí* 拍案惊奇 (*Amazing Tales*, 1628, 1632). More than three hundred different genres of opera (*xìqǔ* 戏曲) developed, combining drama, music, dance, and gorgeous costumes. Some twelve hundred titles are still known and performed.

Scholarship also made its mark. The dictionary *Zìhuì* 字汇 (*Collection of Characters*) by Méi Yīngzuò 梅膺柞 (d. 1615) classified Chinese characters under 214 radicals, the distinctive elements that combine to form complete characters. (The system is still in use.) But no categorization of knowledge can compare with the 11,095-volume *Yǒnglè dàdiǎn* 永乐大典 (*Great Compendium of the Yongle Reign*), the largest "encyclopedia" ever compiled—and it took only five years of intense preparation, from 1403 to 1408, to complete. The term *encyclopedia*, as we know it, doesn't adequately describe the scope of this work, since it included several important texts in the Chinese tradition transcribed in their entirety, and large excerpts from a wide range of others. Some literary, historical, and dramatic works survived only because they were reconstructed or later copied from the *Yongle dadian.* The staff of compilers, editors, and scribes numbered over two thousand, and the table of contents alone filled sixty volumes.

Christian missionary Matteo Ricci (left) greeting the Ming-dynasty scholar-official and Catholic convert Xu Xú Guāngqǐ 徐光启 (right), in a 1669 print. COLLECTION OF THE BEINECKE RARE BOOK AND MANUSCRIPT LIBRARY, YALE UNIVERSITY.

During the Ming, the Chinese increasingly interacted with Europeans, who first appeared in significant numbers in China in 1514. The Europeans came not only to trade but also to convert the local people to Catholicism. The Italian Jesuit Matteo Ricci (Lì Mǎdòu 利玛窦, 1552–1610) was the most successful missionary in China. He introduced the Chinese to some Western scientific and technical knowledge and such mechanical curiosities as clocks. By the time of his death in 1610, Jesuit communities were established in many cities, including Beijing.

The Fall of the Ming (Míngcháo de shuāiluò 明朝的衰落)

For nearly a century after the death of the Yongle emperor in 1424, the Ming dynasty was occasionally threatened by Mongols along the northern frontiers, but still was mostly peaceful and prosperous. In 1449, during a military campaign led by the Ming eunuch Wáng Zhèn 王振, Emperor Yīngzōng 英宗 (1427–1464) was captured and held prisoner by the Oirat (Western Mongols). This incident forced the Ming to focus on defending against the Mongols, which led to the construction of much of the Great Wall that can be seen today. Under Emperor Jiājìng 嘉靖 (1507–1566, reigned from 1522), the Mongols led by Altan Khan 俺答汗 (d. 1583) constantly raided Chinese territory, while Japanese pirates (wōkòu 倭寇) attacked coastal areas at the same time.

The Ming's grand secretary Zhāng Jūzhèng 张居正 (1525–1582) carried out a series of reforms in the late sixteenth century. He centralized the government, repaired the Grand Canal, and limited corrupt practices in civil service examinations. His "single whip" (yī tiáo biān fǎ 一条鞭法) method of taxation made land the sole basis of tax obligations. After Zhang's death, the Ming government again fell into the hands of eunuchs, the most notorious of whom was Wèi Zhōngxián 魏忠贤 (1568–1627). Emperor Chóngzhēn 崇祯 (1611–1644, reigned from 1627) tried to strengthen the Ming but failed because of two developments: peasant rebellions that started in northern Shaanxi (Shǎnxī), and Manchu encroachment from the northeastern frontier. Peasant troops led by Lǐ Zìchéng 李自成 (1605–1645) entered Beijing in April 1644, and Emperor Chongzhen committed suicide. Ming loyalists on the northeast frontier invited the Manchu forces to help suppress the rebels, but when the Manchu entered Beijing in June, they seized the throne for themselves under the dynastic title of Qing.

Qing Dynasty: Manchu Rule

Qīng cháo: Mǎnrén tǒngzhì
清朝: 满人统治
1644–1911/12 (dynasty overthrown
1911, last emperor abdicated 1912)

he Qing, founded by the Manchu in 1644, was the last imperial dynasty to rule China. At its height, it was the largest consolidated empire in Chinese history—and in the world at the time. During its reign the Qing affected great changes in government administration, the economy, regional integration, and intellectual achievement—and it dealt with numerous disasters, both from within China and without. But the Qing could not overcome the movement toward modern nationalism furthered by Sun Yat-sen and his revolutionary followers, a force that helped destroy the old imperial order.

The Manchu were descendants of the Jurchen tribes who controlled north China as the Jurchen Jin dynasty (1125–1234). Their leader, Huáng Tàijí 皇太极 (1592–1643), changed the name of his people from Jurchen to Manchu 满人 in 1635 and the dynastic name from Hòu Jīn 后金 (meaning Later Jin) to Qing 清 (meaning "clear") in 1636. He died in 1643, the year before the Qing became rulers of China.

When the Manchu Qing forces entered Beijing in 1644 under their new six-year-old Emperor Shùnzhì 顺治 (1638–1661, reigned 1644–1661)—who was understandably guided by his uncle, the imperial regent Dorgon 多尔衮 (1612–1650)—they crushed the rebels attempting to overthrow the Ming dynasty, and seized the throne themselves. The Qing established an empire on the Chinese model, with Confucianism as the state orthodoxy, governmental institutions such as the Grand Secretariat and six ministries, and the Ming taxation system. In the Qing government, offices were held by equal numbers of Manchu and Chinese who worked side by side.

During the reigns of emperors Kāngxī 康熙 (reigned 1662–1722) through Qiánlóng 乾隆 (reigned 1735–1795), the Qing reached its height of power and prosperity as the most extensive empire in the world. The Qing subjugated Taiwan in 1683, Outer Mongolia in 1690s, Tibet in 1720, and Xinjiang in 1759.

A portrait of Kangxi in court dress shows the emperor during the height of his (and Qing) power. THE PALACE MUSEUM, BEIJING.

Manchu Identity in a Diverse Empire (Duōyuán dìguó de Mǎnrén tèxìng 多元帝国的满人特性)

As they created a multiethnic empire, the Qing rulers sought to preserve their people's ethnic identity. The Manchu people were urged to retain skills in archery and horsemanship; the Chinese practice of foot binding was prohibited for Manchu women; intermarriage between Manchu and Chinese was prohibited; and the Han Chinese were forbidden from migrating to northeast China. Members of the ruling elite were encouraged to master the Manchu language, and the Manchu were generally granted preferential treatment. In fact, all Han Chinese males were forced to shave the front of their head and wear a braid in the back, a Manchu style that signified political loyalty.

At the same time, the Manchu conquerors did adopt many Chinese values, institutions, and customs. The Qing was a time of intense cultural integration.

The economy thrived under the Qing. Government tax policy aided agricultural and economic development, and instituted measures to benefit poor peasant farmers. China traded with Japan, Southeast Asia, Europe, and the Americas, and foreign trade expanded rapidly in China's favor. China's population also exploded, growing from 150 million at the beginning of the dynasty in the mid-1600s to 360 million in the early 1800s. Part of the reason for this was the prosperity of what was likely then the most dynamic economy in the preindustrial world.

Intellectual and Religious Searching (Xuéshù sīxiǎng yǔ zōngjiào zhuīqiú 学术思想与宗教追求)

In the early Qing, the Manchu declared neo-Confucianism the state orthodoxy. In order to control intellectuals and the spread of knowledge, the Qing state sponsored enormous literary projects, such as the *Gǔjīn túshū jíchéng* 古今图书集成 (*Synthesis of Books and Illustrations Past and Present, 1726–1728*). Many scholars devoted themselves to the laborious literary work known as the *kǎozhèngxué* 考证学 ("evidential research movement"), which contributed hugely to critical studies of Chinese history, philosophy, and philology. Literary works such as *Liáozhāi zhìyì* 聊斋志异 (*Strange Tales from a Chinese Studio*) by Pú Sōnglíng 蒲松龄 (1640–1715), *Rúlín wàishǐ* 儒林外史 (*The Scholars*) by Wú Jìngzǐ (1701–1754), and *Hónglóu mèng* 红楼梦 (*Dream of the Red Chamber*) by Cáo Xuěqín 曹雪芹 (1715–1763), vividly exposed the social problems of their times.

European missionaries continued to work at the imperial court and in the provinces. During the nineteenth century, Protestant missionaries brought Western values, science, technology, medicine, and education to China. By the end of the century, there were about 750 Catholic and 1,300 Protestant missionaries in China, who converted about 200,000 Chinese.

Conflict Within and Without (Nèidòu yǔ wàizhēng 内斗与外争)

The nineteenth century also brought a number of struggles with Western powers that led to the decline of the Qing dynasty. The First Opium War (1839–1842) began with increasing frictions about foreign trade: Chinese attempts to restrict British merchants to certain Chinese ports, to demand payment for Chinese luxury goods like tea and silk in silver currency, and to prohibit British importation of opium. After China's defeat, the Treaty of Nanjing ceded Hong Kong to the British, and China was forced to open ports to foreign trade in certain coastal cities—where foreign imperialist powers were granted political, economic, and legal privileges unfavorable to the Chinese.

Opium trade continued and grew, and so did the problems caused by the war and the resulting treaty ports: China's deep humiliation at the hands of European powers and the residual anger many Chinese felt for a Manchu government who seemed helpless to overcome it. Such were the underlying causes of the Taiping Rebellion (*Tàipíng qǐyì* 太平起义), which lasted from 1851 to 1864 and—claiming the lives of 20 to 30 million Chinese by its end—turned into the most devastating of all civil wars worldwide. The catalyst for the rebellion was actually Hóng Xiùquán 洪秀全, who, having repeatedly failed the provincial-level civil service examinations, got involved with a Baptist missionary from Tennessee; Hong then became convinced he was actually Jesus Christ's younger brother, sent to Earth to expel devils, namely the Manchu, from China. Other large popular uprisings included the Nián Rebellion 捻军起义 (1853–1868) in the east and the Muslim rebellion (1855–1873) in Yunnan. None of these rebellions overthrew the Qing dynasty, but they weakened it and led to a shift in power, from the Manchu central government to members of the provincial Chinese elite.

Attempts at Revival (**Yìyù fùxīng** 意欲复兴)

After the Opium War, the political and intellectual elite in China looked to the West for ideas to enrich the country and strengthen the military. Their attitudes, however, involved less than admiration for the ways of the West; instead they seemed to be looking for ways to "fight fire with fire." Wèi Yuán 魏源 (1794–1856), for example, a scholar who passed his first civil service examinations at age fourteen and went on to become an editor and author, claimed that he wanted to present educated Chinese with a realistic representation of the outside world. In his famous *Hǎiguó túzhì* 海国图志 (*Illustrated Treatise on Overseas Countries*), he suggested that Western barbarians, in their quest for profit and power, had engineered techniques and machines to conquer the civilized world—and China, although committed to spiritual and moral virtue, learning, and peace, would be well served to analyze those techniques and use them to triumph over the enemy.

A similar mindset was in play during China's Self-Strengthening Movement (Yángwù yùndòng 洋务运动, 1861–1895), one in a series of modernization programs the Qing instituted to revive the empire. The government sponsored a number of "self-strengthening" projects designed to bolster the navy. The idea was to adopt Western technology but not the values and philosophies that produced it—China would learn from the West, equal it, and then surpass it. Despite good intentions to beef up a military industrial complex, the Qing's refusal to alter its system of government and its

Ruling from Behind the Curtain

Empress Dowager Cixi 慈禧太后 *(1835–1908) held great power over Qing political life for almost fifty years—especially over her nephew, Emperor Guangxu.*

Cixi (nee Yehonala), born into the Manchu Blue Banner (an elite group under the Qing) became a consort of Emperor Xian Feng 咸丰 (ruled 1850–1861). She gave birth to his successor, Tongzhi, in 1856. After Xian Feng's death in 1861, Cixi set herself up as the sole regent over the boy. In 1875, Tongzhi died with no heir; Cixi named her three-year-old nephew Guangxu (ruled 1875–1908) to the throne.

In 1898, Cixi staged a coup to stop Guangxu's proposals for modernization, put him under palace arrest, and ruled, as the Chinese say, "from behind the curtain." Involvement in the Boxer movement led to her declaration of war against foreign powers and the humiliating 1901 treaty known as the Boxer Protocol—after which she implemented (ironically, considering her former anti-modernization stance), the beginnings of a Chinese constitution.

Imperial officials immediately attributed Guangxu's sudden death on 14 November 1908 to natural causes, but rumors of foul play swirled inside and outside palace walls, especially after Cixi died twenty-two hours later. Now scientific analyses of the emperor's hair and bones revealed that he died of acute arsenic poisoning. National Public Radio's Louisa Lim broadcast the story on the hundred-year anniversary of Guangxu's death. She interviewed Zhu Chenru, deputy director of the National Committee for the Compilation of Qing History, whose institute carried out the tests over a five-year period with other Chinese agencies. On one 10-inch-long hair they found arsenic content 2,400 times higher than normal. Scientists ruled out environmental factors or chronic poisoning over time due to traces of arsenic in traditional medicines. Two mysteries remained: motive and murderer.

Zhu's familiarity with Qing records makes him a modern-day palace insider. He believes Cixi worried that Guangxu would instigate radical reform if he survived her, that Cixi was the mastermind, and that her cronies carried out the plot. (Anecdotal evidence points to a court eunuch of Cixi's, who was seen coming from her quarters with a bowl of yogurt and instructions to take it to the emperor. Two hours later, someone heard weeping and shouts that the emperor was dead.)

A U.S. Qing historian, Joseph Esherick, spoke to Lim about the impact of (and Chinese interest in) the findings. Numerous newspaper articles in China questioned whether the country might have become a

Ruling from Behind the Curtain (*continued*)

constitutional monarchy had Guangxu not been murdered, reflecting a yearning, he said, to add a story of reform within the system to the history of modern China. For the Chinese Qing historian, the symbolism was quite different. A hundred years ago ordinary people weren't even allowed to look at Guangxu. But now an ordinary person like Zhu can touch his bones.

Source: Louisa Lim. (2008, November 14). *Who Murdered China's Emperor 100 Years?* Retrieved December 6, 2009, from http://www.npr.org/templates/story/story.php?storyId=96993694

---

social hierarchy had a weakening effect exposed by China's defeat in the First Sino-Japanese War (1894–1895).

The Foreign Affairs Movement (Yángwù yùndòng 洋务运动), another valiant effort aimed at Qing revival, occurred during the reigns of Tóngzhì 同治 (r. 1862–1874) and Guāngxù 光绪 (r. 1875–1908), both of whom were actually controlled by Tongzhi's mother, Cíxǐ 慈禧 (1835–1898). Under the principle of *zhōngxué wéitǐ, xīxué wéiyòng* 中学为体, 西学为用 ("Chinese learning as the essence and Western learning as practical use"), the Qing state promoted industrial development that included building arsenals, machine factories, schools, railways, shipyards, telegraph lines, and postal services, as well as a modern army and navy.

The Foreign Affairs Movement did help to modernize China but not sufficiently to fight off the encroachments of Western powers. In the Sino-French War of 1884–1885, China lost Vietnam. In 1887, China officially ceded the long lost Macao to Portugal. During the Sino-Japanese War of 1894–1895, Japan defeated China and forced it to recognize Korean independence and to cede Taiwan to Japan. (Because relations between Japan and China faltered on and off from ancient times, and the memories of Japanese piracy in the Ming maritime era were still vivid, Chinese defeat by Japan was far more humiliating, and would continue to be so until the mid-twentieth century, than defeat by Western powers.) Foreign powers began scrambling for concessions, areas of land that were leased in perpetuity, in China.

In 1898, there emerged a new movement called Bǎi rì wéi xīn 百日维新 (Hundred Days of Reform). A group of intellectuals persuaded Emperor Guangxu to call for changes in education, political administration, industry, and foreign relations. Opposed by the powerful Empress Dowager Cixi, the movement had few positive results. (For more on Cixi and Guangxu, see the sidebar "Ruling Behind the Curtain.")

The End of the Empire (Dìguó mòrì 帝国末日)

In the late 1890s, a secret society in China called the Boxers United in Righteousness (Yìhétuán 义和团) arose. This group blamed Christian converts and foreign establishments for the worsening condition of the common people in China. The Boxers practiced martial arts alongside altars or in boxing grounds, and they believed their training, along with charms and spells, would make them invulnerable to bullets. In 1900, the Qing court began to support them, and the Boxers attacked the foreign legations in Beijing. The uprising was put down by a military alliance of eight countries known to the Chinese as Bā guó liánjūn (八国联军). They ransacked parts of Beijing and forced the Qing to pay huge reparations and accept the establishment of foreign military guards in Beijing. To preserve its commercial interests in China, the United

---

Damage incurred by the Boxer Rebellion, and later during the Cultural Revolution, left much of the Qing Summer Palace, the Yuanming Yuan, in ruins.

States announced the Open Door policy (Ménhù kāifàng 门户开放政策) and requested that all countries not deny others access to their spheres of influence.

The Qing's failure to deal effectively with these crises stimulated Han-Chinese nationalism. The Gémìng jūn 革命军 (The Revolutionary Army) under Zōu Róng 邹容 called on the Chinese to reject Manchu rule in 1903. The Nationalists, led by Sun Yat-sen 孙逸仙, known in China as Sūn Zhōngshān 孙中山, (1866–1925) looked to political revolution as the solution.

During the first decade of the twentieth century, the Qing court engaged in more radical reforms. It was too little, too late. In 1905, the age-old civil service examination system was abolished. Thousands of Chinese students were sent to study abroad. The government and its legal institutions were modernized. In 1908, the court issued the Xiànfǎ dàgāng 宪法大纲 (Outline of Constitution). This introduced constitutional monarchy to China and defined the "rights and responsibilities" of the people. Provincial assemblies were established in 1909, and a consultative national assembly in 1910. The revolutionaries were not satisfied. The 1911 Revolution (Xīnhài gémìng 辛亥革命) resulted in the founding of a new government—the Republic of China (Zhōnghuá mínguó 中华民国). The last emperor of the Qing, who reigned as Xuāntǒng 宣统 and is better known as Pǔyí 溥仪, formally abdicated on 12 February 1912. (He died in 1967.) Four thousand years after it started, China's dynastic system came to a close.

Sun Yat-sen (Sūn Zhōngshān 孙中山)

Sun Yat-sen (1866–1925) was born to a farming family near Guangzhou (Canton) and received a medical degree in Hong Kong. His English name comes from his original name Sun Yixian 孙逸仙 (spoken in Cantonese as Sun Yat-sen), but he is in fact better known in China by his revolutionary name of Sun Zhongshan 孙中山.

In 1879, thirteen-year-old Sun went to Hawaii to live with his elder brother. There he studied English in a private school operated by Christian missionaries. After returning to China he decided to study Western medicine in Guangzhou (Canton) and Hong Kong, but he quickly put aside his career as a doctor for politics.

China had been weakened and humiliated by Western imperialism, and at first Sun tried working with Qing officials to strengthen the country the affect reform. But working within the government brought no change, and in 1894 he organized the Revive China Society (Xīngzhōnguì 兴中会) among overseas Chinese with the goal of expelling the "foreign" Manchus of the Qing dynasty and forming a republic. He traveled extensively among Chinese communities in North America, Southeast Asia, and Japan, tirelessly promoting the revolutionary cause. He called his ideals for the republic the Three People's Principles (Sānmín zhǔyì 三民主义):

nationalism, democracy, and the livelihood of the people (perhaps an echo of Abraham Lincoln's famous "of the people, by the people, and for the people" theme). In 1904, Sun Yat-sen somehow obtained a birth certificate stating that he was born in Waimano on the island of Oahu, and thereby became naturalized as a U.S. citizen. He later explained his U.S. citizenship made it easier to carry on the revolution overseas.

Sun Yat-sen became an icon for his patriotism and for his goals toward building a strong, modernized China; Chinese scholars often treat him as a sacred figure. His critics, many of them in the West, tend to view Sun as a man who advocated change but was never able to execute it. But part of Sun's legacy—especially his role in linking China to overseas Chinese communities and his advocacy of industrial development—can be seen as prophetic of China's place in the current globalizing world.

Sun was temporarily buried in the Biyun Temple 碧云寺 in Beijing. In 1929 Sun's body was moved to a magnificently designed mausoleum built in a huge cemetery park in Nanjing. Some 5 meters (16.4 feet) underneath a sarcophagus that supports a marble statue of Sun, he lies at rest in an American-made copper coffin.

Chapter 3: A Century of Change—From 1912 to Today

1912 nián zhì jīn de bǎi nián biànhuà 1912
年至今的百年变化

*I*f we were to stage a drama based on China's history over the last century—beginning with the fall of the Qīng 清 dynasty in 1911 and the abdication of the last emperor in 1912—the synopsis in our playbill might read something like this:

Act I: The Nationalist Party, led by Sun Yat-sen 孙逸仙, takes center stage in 1911 as it establishes the Republic of China. For the next thirty-seven years, the Nationalists strive to control this vast country, contending with feuding warlords, a bitter rivalry with Chinese Communists, military struggles with Japan, and a significant, mostly offstage relationship with the Soviet Union.

Act II: The Chinese Communist Party, under Máo Zédōng 毛泽东, triumphs in 1949 and establishes the People's Republic. The next twenty-seven years of Mao's rule are filled with gripping events—grand programs to transform the country, purges in party leadership, famines, and Red Guard uprisings, to name just a few.

Act III: After Mao's death in 1976, the next three decades are marked by gradual political changes—and dramatic economic ones—beginning with Vice Premier Deng Xiaoping's four cardinal principles and his formula for moving China ahead in four areas (agriculture, industry, science and technology, and defense). In the 1990s China's leadership passes to a new generation; China finds more stability and begins to realize some of its enormous potential. Can China truly take the leading role it seeks on the world stage?

In this chapter, we'll bring the history of China up to date and help you understand why today China is so often in the spotlight.

China as a Republic
(Gònghé de Zhōngguó 共和的中国)
(1911/12–1949)

*B*y the end of the nineteenth century, just about every political and intellectual leader in China saw the need for change. Some, such as Sun Yat-
sen, felt that rather than reforming the imperial system, China needed a
complete revolution. Sun was exiled from the country by the Qing government, but
his followers succeeded in infiltrating the military and spreading his revolutionary ideals—although the ten uprisings they attempted between 1895 and 1911 were
unsuccessful.

On 9 October 1911, an accidental explosion rocked the revolutionaries' secret headquarters in Hànkǒu 汉口. Police raided the building and discovered, along with a stash
of weapons, the membership rolls that listed those loyal to the revolution. Knowing
that their identities were revealed, soldiers faithful to Sun quickly mutinied. By the
afternoon of 10 October, a day known as *shuāng shí* 双十 ("double tenth"), they had
captured the entire city of Hankou. Within weeks, province after province declared its
independence from Běijīng.

The Betrayal of the Revolution
(Pànbiàn gémìng 叛变革命)

Sun Yat-sen had been raising funds for the revolution in Denver, Colorado, at the time
of the initial explosion. He returned to China, and on 29 December 1911 he was elected
provisional president of the new Republic. The Qing emperor, however, refused to give
up the throne.

Not being a strong military leader, Sun sought the support of Yuán Shìkǎi
袁世凯, a Qing general who had worked toward reforming the imperial system during its last years, and who, in 1911, had been in charge of negotiations between Qing
troops and the revolutionaries. Yuan's immense military power allowed him to manip-
ulate both sides—in February 1912, Sun and the Qing court simultaneously appointed

Yuan as president, and the emperor agreed to abdicate.

In 1913 Yuan betrayed the revolution by disbanding the parliament and calling for a new constitution. He declared Sun's revolutionary party illegal, forcing Sun into exile once again. In 1915 Yuan assembled his own

---

Topics for Further Study

May Fourth Movement

New Culture Movement

Sun Yat-sen

Yuan Shikai

---

special "representative assembly," which voted unanimously to make Yuan emperor as of 1 January 1916. Within a few months, a rebellion against this return to monarchy broke out in the southern provinces, Yuan's ceremonial induction was cancelled, and he died soon after in the summer of 1916.

Even after Yuan's death, Sun and his followers lacked the power to bring back the Republican government they founded in 1912. For the next decade, from 1917 to 1927, China fell into a state of perpetual disorder. Incessant fighting, spawned by military commanders who took control in different parts of the country, allowed numerous foreign powers to take advantage of China's disunity by establishing their spheres of influence along the Chinese coast.

The May Fourth Movement (Wǔ sì yùndòng 五四运动)

Intellectuals during these years wanted China's culture, especially its language and literature, to be rejuvenated just as much as they wanted Chinese government and politics to be democratized. In 1915 a new journal was launched in Shànghǎi—*Xīn qīngnián* 新青年 (*New Youth*)—that spurred young urban Chinese to adopt a more modern worldview. Its editor, Chén Dúxiù 陈独秀 (1879–1942), argued that many of China's backward practices could be eliminated or reformed with the assistance of Dé xiānsheng (Mr. Democracy) and Sài xiānsheng (Mr. Science). Chen urged the upcoming generation of intellectuals to turn their backs on traditional Confucian values of filial piety, hierarchy, and ritual—they were regressive and antimodern, he wrote—and embrace instead cosmopolitan, progressive, and utilitarian ideas. (Chen established his own rebellious tradition as a student in Japan: he was asked to leave the country in 1903 when he snipped off a Chinese official's queue—the braid of hair usually worn hanging at the back of the head. The act symbolized his disrespect for the ineffective and corrupt Qing court.) Chen's publication "took off" among students within months. Many historians see Chen and *New Youth* as the catalysts for what would eventually be called the May Fourth Movement (Wǔ sì yùndòng 五四运动), an era that lasted from about 1915 to 1923, as well as the New Culture Movement (Xīn wén huà yùndòng 新文化运动).

In 1917 Chen became the dean of the School of Letters at Peking (Beijing) University, a hotbed of intellectual activity among students, faculty members, and independent writers. There he met Hú Shì 胡适 (1891–1962), a young professor with a U.S. education and the conviction that literature was at the heart of China's cultural problems. China's classical written language, with its highly specialized, obscure vocabulary and its terse structure, was inaccessible to all but the most educated people, and Hu believed that writing in the vernacular would open China's world of letters to those with a more rudimentary education. Hu made pointed suggestions for writers in the pages of *New Youth*: discard stale literary phrases, avoid classical allusions, and stop imitating the ancients. Only writers true to their feelings, he said, would produce something with substance and meaning. Indeed, the focus on vernacular (*báihuà* 白话) literature sparked a greater democratization of China's literary scene.

The May Fourth Movement's political aspect began most decisively with, and gained its name from, the demonstrations of 4 May 1919. On that day crowds of irate students, educators, and urban workers converged on Beijing's Tiān'ānmén Square to protest the Paris Peace Conference. The victors (Allies) of World War I had organized the conference, which continued for months, in part to negotiate treaties distributing former German- or Ottoman-held territories. Concern among Chinese sprung up about what would happen to territories that had once belonged to them, especially since they had been under Japanese control since within weeks of the war's beginning in August 1914, when Japan declared war on Germany. China had eventually joined the Allied forces against Germany in 1917, and many Chinese, encouraged by the call for "self-determination" and "territorial integrity" in U.S. president Woodrow Wilson's Fourteen Points speech, assumed they would regain control over those territories after the war. The Chinese delegates attending the peace conference certainly thought so, and they were stunned when Japan's delegates revealed several agreements made among Britain, France, and Italy that honored Japan's demands in China.

The crowds marching through Beijing's streets on 4 May denounced Japan's underhanded tactics and demanded that China's representatives reject the agreements, but government troops suppressed the demonstration within hours. Despite ongoing protests, the Treaty of Versailles, signed on 28 June 1919, allowed Japan to retain control over the Chinese territory. The refusal of the Chinese delegates to sign the treaty marked a significant moment in the development of Chinese nationalism. In the days after 4 May, more protests erupted throughout China. Today 4 May is commemorated as Youth Day, and intellectuals involved in the movement are celebrated as patriotic heroes.

Those in the May Fourth Movement became increasingly obsessed by ideologies in the years after 1919. A number of "isms"—socialism, anarchism, syndicalism (a revolutionary doctrine by which workers seize control of the economy and the government by direct means), and even pragmatism—competed for attention. During the summer of 1921, a group of young intellectuals held a meeting in Shànghǎi to found the Chinese Communist Party (CCP). Among its founding members were Chen Duxiu and, significantly, Mao Zedong, who would soon become the most iconic of twentieth-century China's revolutionaries.

Reuniting China (Tǒngyī Zhōngguó 统一中国)

During this time of cultural change and political turmoil, Sun Yat-sen retreated to his home in Guǎngzhōu (Canton), where in 1923 he reorganized his Nationalist Party (Guómíndǎng 国民党) Leninist-style—with a clear ideology, a limited membership under firm party discipline, and a strong army under party control. (Lenin believed that strong political leaders [dictators] were the real driving force behind revolution, not the uprisings of the working class.) This meant that the Nationalists resembled not only the Soviet Communists, but, ironically, the Chinese Communists who would defeat them a few decades later.

From his experience with Yuan Shikai, Sun Yat-sen realized the importance of having reliable military backing, so he established the Huángpǔjūnxiào 黄埔军校 (Whampoa Military Academy) to train loyal troops. The head of this academy was a young soldier named Chiang Kai-shek 蒋介石 (Jiǎng Jièshí in pinyin, 1887–1975), who quickly rose in power among the Nationalists. The Western powers were not willing to help the Nationalists in their goal of reunifying China, so Sun turned to the Soviet Union for help. The Soviets agreed to offer aid, seeing the Nationalists as one stage (the "bourgeois" one) in a revolution that would eventually lead to a Communist China. In 1923, Sun and the Nationalists agreed to form a "united front" with the new Chinese Communist Party (CCP) in order to rid China of warlords and to establish a stable government.

Sun Yat-sen died in 1925, and Chiang Kai-shek became the leader of the Nationalists. In 1926 he launched the Northern Expedition (Běifá 北伐), a military campaign to unite the entire country under Guomindang rule. With Russian aid, Chiang's forces soon put much of China under Nationalist control. At about the same time, Chiang renounced any continued cooperation with the Chinese Communists. In 1927 the Nationalists brutally suppressed Shanghai's Communist-led labor movement and after that Chiang sought to destroy all traces of the CCP. Some Communists went underground, and some, led by Mao Zedong and other leaders, retreated into the mountainous countryside in Jiāngxī Province to establish the Jiangxi Soviet Republic. By 1928 Chiang had eliminated or weakened both the warlords and the Communists, and China was once again reunited.

Water and the Way (*Dao*)

Throughout China's history rulers sought guidance from philosophers on matters of statecraft and administration; Confucian thought undoubtedly dominated the field of the civil service examinations during imperial China. In 1905 the Qing government (1644–1911/12) abolished the exams, one of several steps in a last-ditch effort to appeal to a restless populace moving toward modernity, but the dynasty's efforts at reform were too little too late. Two decades after the founding of Republican China, its Nationalist leaders found themselves losing support of the peasant class, which accounted for the majority of China's population. They might have benefited from reading the Laozi.

In teaching about the Way (*dao*), the *Laozi* advises the wise ruler who wants to bring peace and harmony to the masses: Don't micromanage affairs of state, just emulate the forces of nature. A related concept involves "acting by not acting" (*wéi wú wéi* 为无为). "Not acting," according to the *Laozi*, does not mean doing nothing at all, but acting naturally, without resistance to nature. Chapter 78 of the *Laozi* explains how water, which nourishes all things without discriminating between them, is the model of nature:

There is nothing in the world softer and weaker than water, but for attacking the solid and strong, there is nothing better. Nothing can substitute for it. That the weak can overcome the strong and the soft can overcome the solid, everyone in the world knows this, but none can put it into practice. Therefore the sage has said, "To receive the dirt of a country is to be the lord of its altars of soil and grain. To bear the suffering of a country is to be the king of the world." Truth sounds contradictory.

Source: Philip J. Ivanhoe. (2002). *The daodejing of Laozi* (p. 81). New York: Seven Bridges Press.

Japanese troops enter Shenyang, Manchuria in 1931. Japan's militarism after the Manchurian Incident dashed any remaining hopes that the Chinese Nationalists could build a strong central government.

The Decade of Republican Rule
(Gònghé shí nián 共和十年)

From 1928 to 1937, Chiang Kai-shek and the Nationalists ruled over China from their capital in Nánjīng; this period is sometimes called the "Nanjing Decade." Having established control, Chiang and his associates were able to implement the republican ideas of Sun Yat-sen. With the Communists out of the way, the Nationalists formed a one-party dictatorship, allegedly seeking to make the country ready for democracy.

Guomindang leaders worked from Nanjing to strengthen China domestically and internationally. The government took control of four national banks and introduced monetary reform. The Ministry of Education created or reorganized twenty-two universities, and the Ministry of Transportation extended railways, opened new highways, and created domestic airline routes. By 1931, Chiang's ministers had some successes on the international front, as China regained control over trade tariffs and revoked many foreign concessions, thereby ending some policies that had humiliated China at the hands of Western powers for decades.

During their nine years of control, the Nationalists made only spotty progress in improving agricultural production. Even with the improvements in education, finance, and communications, most people in China saw very little change in their daily lives. The peasantry comprising about 80 percent of the population could have benefited from land reform and rent reduction. The Nationalists, though, concentrated on the needs of the urban middle class. As a result, many peasants looked instead to the Communists for relief.

Despite its rigorous Leninist-style rule, the Nationalists couldn't manage to suppress all the differing agendas within its ranks. Chiang Kai-shek was good at manipulating factions but never able to achieve total control. In the cities, the Nationalists made alliances with bosses deeply involved in illegal activities; in rural areas, they had few effective programs or influential allies. The government at Nanjing had succeeded in uniting China but only with limited territorial control and many weaknesses.

The Manchurian Incident
(Mǎnzhóulǐ shìbiàn 满洲里事变)

The Nationalist government might have eventually been successful in developing a strong central government and modernizing China. Rising Japanese militarism, though, helped to quash whatever chance the Nationalists may have had.

In September 1931, the Japanese army forces stationed in Kwantung (Guāndōng 关东), a northeastern area of China, claimed that Chinese bandits had sabotaged the Japanese-controlled South Manchuria Railway outside Fèngtiān 奉天 (today's

Shěnyáng 沈阳) in the southern part of northeast China. Although Japanese trains traveled the railway soon after the rather dubious "explosion," Japanese forces used what became known as the Manchurian Incident (Mǎnzhóulǐ shìbiàn 满洲事变)—known to the Chinese as Jiǔyībā shìbiàn 九一八事变 (the September 18th Incident)—as an excuse for a year-long campaign to gain control over all of Manchuria.

The Chinese government complained to the League of Nations, which appointed a commission of inquiry that strongly criticized the Japanese. In response, Japan withdrew from the League and eventually tried to demonstrate Manchurian "independence" by establishing a puppet government over what it called Manchukuo 满洲国 (Manchu country). The leader the Japanese installed in 1932 was Pǔyí 溥仪, the last Qing emperor. Throughout the 1930s, Japanese military forces took one Chinese province after another and eventually widened the war into Southeast Asia, a turn of events that would greatly influence things throughout the Pacific—including, on a December morning a few years later, what happened at the U.S. naval base on the Hawaiian island of Oahu, the Pearl Harbor.

The Long March (Chángzhēng 长征)

Besides contending with the Japanese in the 1930s, Chiang Kai-shek and the Nationalists were also in a continuing struggle with the Chinese Communist Party (CCP). After the bloody purge by the Nationalists in 1927, the CCP relocated their base from Shanghai to form an enclave in Jiangxi Province called the Jiangxi Soviet Republic. A significant party leader as he was, Mao Zedong was not as influential as the Twenty-Eight Bolsheviks (Èrshíbā ge Bùérshíwéikè 二十八个布尔什维克), a name for a group of Moscow-trained CCP leaders. They believed, as the Soviets now did, under Joseph Stalin, that urban workers would lead the eventual revolution in China. Mao, on the other hand, held that the revolution would rely on the peasantry, the vast majority of Chinese in this era. Mao certainly had a point. In the regions they controlled, the Communist leaders took over and redistributed land, gaining the support of the poor peasants and increasing the popularity of the CCP in these regions.

Throughout the early 1930s, Chiang and his forces waged four failed campaigns to encircle and eradicate the Chinese Communists. In October 1933, the Nationalists gave it a fifth try. With advice from German experts, the Nationalist forces mobilized 700,000 men to build a series of cement blockhouses around the Communist troops in Jiangxi. As a result of the military conflicts and economic blockade about a million

Topics for Further Study

Manchurian Incident

Mao Zedong

Chinese Communist Party (CCP)

people died. In early 1934, Mao, who had advocated guerrilla warfare techniques, was removed from his position in the CCP leadership, and by mid-1934 the Communist Red Army was defeated.

Mao and the Chinese Communists survived this desperate situation by beginning a retreat, known as the Long March (Chángzhēng 长征), an event that became a legendary part of Chinese history. On 15 October 1934, 86,000 Communist military personnel, along with 30,000 party officials and members, broke through the blockade in Jiangxi and fled westward. In the first three months the Communists, led by Zhū Dé 朱德 (1886–1976) and Zhōu Ēnlái 周恩来 (1898–1976), were frequently bombarded and attacked by the Nationalist forces and suffered great losses. As the march continued to the northwest, Mao's tactics of guerrilla warfare were gradually adopted. When the Communists reached Zūnyì 遵义, Guìzhōu Province, in early 1935, Mao had gathered enough support to establish his dominance over the Soviet-trained faction.

Under Mao's leadership, the Communists proceeded toward Shaanxi (Shǎnxī 陕西) via a mountainous and sometimes marshy and snow-clad route with no signs of human habitation and scarce resources. In October 1935, the Red Army arrived at Shaanxi in Northwest China. The troops had crossed eighteen mountain ranges and twenty-four rivers in 370 days for a total journey of 12,500 kilometers, about 7,767 miles.

In his famous 1935 book *Red Star Over China*, Edgar Snow attributes Mao himself as the source for this distance, but two British researchers, Ed Jocelyn and Andrew McEwen, authors of the 2003 book *The Long March*, explain how they retraced the route and estimate the march to have covered only 6,000 kilometers, or about 3,700 miles. No doubt the route was winding, and Jocelyn and McEwen speculate that Mao might have further "twisted" the tale of the march to suit his own purposes. The Chinese media stick by Mao's figure, however, saying it is an unchallengeable part of the historical record. Still, to consider what the Long March was like, imagine making a year long, off-road survival hike through the most treacherous terrain from New York City to Los Angeles—and making the trek back, going with Mao's numbers. It was an incredible achievement, but not everyone survived it. The Communist contingent of more than 100,000 fleeing Jiangxi was down to about 8,000 marching into Shaanxi. New recruits had been added on the way, but many of them died. Some left to mobilize the peasantry en route, others just quit.

In the middle of 1936, the remnants of several Red Army troops gathered in northern Shaanxi, with Yán'ān 延安 as their headquarters. By the end of the year, the Red Army was 30,000 strong, more than triple its size at the end of the march, and yet only a third of its former number. The remoteness and difficult terrain of the area survived

A Communist cadre leader addresses survivors of the Long March.

it easier for the Communists to defend themselves against the Nationalists and gave them another chance to regroup.

After the Long March, a number of things changed for the Communists. The party had gained local peasant support during the march, and the dwindling of foreign Communist influence encouraged a homegrown, Chinese Communist doctrine that was adapted to China's unique historical circumstances and its economic situation. But most significantly, Mao had become the supreme leader, and Zhou Enlai was installed as his unquestioning right-hand man—a situation that changed little over the next forty years.

The Xi'an Incident (Xī'ān shìbiàn 西安事变)

Besides running the Communists out of Jiangxi, what else were the Nationalists doing in this period? In the 1930s, as fascism rose in Europe, Chiang Kai-shek promoted some fascist-style organizations, such as the Blue Shirts (Lányīshè 蓝衣社), a group of ultranationalist young men with a name and purpose similar to that of the Brown Shirts, the brutal supporters of Mussolini's regime in Italy. Also in the fascist style, Chiang's regime took greater control over business in the country and reined in the media to avoid any criticism. The Nationalists had become the head of another old-style bureaucracy, one not really in touch with the people of the country.

After the Long March, the CCP called for all the warring factions in China to unite against Japanese aggression. Chiang, however, saw the Communists as a greater

Family Ties

Some historians have faulted Chiang Kai-shek for failing to bring about the democracy he promised China, for his conservatism and corruption, and for his lack of concern about the populace. Unlike Mao Zedong, Chiang was not an easily likeable, charismatic figure, and despite his army career, he was a poor field commander. He operated through trusted cronies and family members, often prizing loyalty above competence.

Such criticism contains a measure of truth. But recent scholarly writing on Chiang has tended to re-evaluate him and his era. (See Jay Taylor's 2009 biography, *The Generalissimo: Chiang Kai-shek and the Struggle for Modern China*.) Chiang's two decades of administration based in Nanjing were an exceptionally testing time, marked by invasion, regional strife, economic difficulties, and the challenges of modernization. Through it all, Chiang did indeed get by, with a little help from his family (and friends).

When Chiang married Soong Mei-ling (宋美齡), the younger daughter of the late Shanghai tycoon (and Methodist minister) Charlie Soong (宋耀如), the couple declared that theirs was a marriage of love rather than of political ambition. (Charlie's second daughter, Soong Qing-ling (宋慶齡), was the widow of Sun Yat-sen.) But the marriage was quite a triumph for the country boy from Xikou (Fenghua, Zhejiang Province). It brought him into contact with two of China's leading political and business figures. The first was Mei-ling's brother, Soong Ziwen (宋子文), known in the West as T. V. Soong, and the second was Mei-ling's brother-in-law Kong Xiangxi (孔祥熙)—also called H. H. Kung—who was married to the eldest of Soong Ziwen's three sisters. Both men were wealthy bankers and businessmen; each would become China's prime minister and finance minister in turn.

Soong Mei-ling, popularly known as Madame Chiang, later played a pivotal role in Chiang's life and politics. She negotiated his release from a 1936 military coup staged by Zhang Xueliang (张学良) and in 1943 lobbied both the U.S. Senate and House of Representatives for military aid. She endorsed Chiang's New Life Movement (新生活运动), designed to revitalize the spirit of the people by encouraging traditional ethics and behavior modification as a way of improving their living habits. Controversy surrounds the rationale behind the New Life Movement: some thought it stemmed from Confucian and Christian ideals; other thought it too close for comfort to fascism.

After the exile of the Chiang's Nationalist Party to the island of Taiwan (Republic of China), Chiang vowed to fight Communism. He imposed martial law, limiting civil

---

Family Ties (continued)

liberties like free speech and the right to form opposition political parties. He died in 1975, still among a powerful network of supporters, without realizing his dream of winning back the mainland from Mao.

Adapted in part from "Chiang Kai-shek," by Jonathan Fenby, from forthcoming (2010) Berkshire Dictionary of Chinese Biography.

---

threat and wanted to destroy them once and for all before dealing with the Japanese. But many Nationalists agreed with the CCP's call for a united front, including two generals: Zhāng Xuéliáng 张学良, the young commander of strong warlord army from Manchuria, and Yáng Hǔchéng 杨虎城, a former bandit leading more dubious troops. Both men, based in Xī'ān, opted to focus on the Japanese incursion in northeast China instead of fighting the Red Army in mid-western China. When, in late 1936, Chiang ordered Zhang and Yang to attack the weakened Communists in hopes of dealing them a final blow, both generals ignored his command. Chiang flew to their headquarters in Xi'an on 3 December 1936 to pressure them personally and rouse the armies. Nine days later, at the start of what became known as the Xi'an Incident (Xī'ān shìbiàn 西安事变), Zhang's forces kidnapped Chiang and put him under house arrest. (An account of the event by the historian Jonathan Fenby describes an almost slapstick scene: when Chiang tried to flee by climbing out the window of his hotel room—leaving his false teeth behind—he fell into a moat, injured his back, and hobbled up a snow-covered hill to hide in a cave, where he eventually gave himself up.)

Although the capture of Chiang initially pleased the Chinese Communists, they were encouraged by the Communists in Moscow not to support Zhang but to work instead for Chiang's release. (Joseph Stalin, it seems, liked Chiang better than any other Chinese leader.) The CCP sent Zhou Enlai to Xi'an to strike a bargain with General Zhang: release Chiang if he promises to work with the CCP against the Japanese. Zhang—further persuaded by Madame Chiang (Sòng Měi-líng 宋美龄), who had flown over from Nanjing to make her husband's case—agreed to release Chiang. In return, Chiang acquiesced, just a bit grudgingly under house arrest: the Nationalists and the CCP would maintain a united front against Japan.

But the plot thickened when Chiang convinced Zhang and Yang to return with him to Nanjing. There, with the tables turned, Chiang put Zhang under house arrest and had Yang executed. (When the Nationalists eventually retreated to Taiwan after the Communists established the People's Republic of China in 1949, Zhang Xueliang was taken with them, where he continued to live under house arrest until 1991. Zhang then moved to Hawaii and died there in 2001, at age one hundred.)

In the aftermath of the Xi'an Incident, the Nationalists and the Communists forged another unwilling alliance in the interest of a united China, an alliance that worked tenuously until the reason for it—the occupation of the Japanese—was no longer a factor.

The War with Japan and the Chinese Civil War

(Kàngzhàn yǔ Nèizhàn 抗战与内战) 1937–1949

By 1937, after Chiang Kai-shek had reluctantly agreed to cooperate with the Communist Party to confront Japanese troops, war with Japan seemed inevitable. A minor clash outside Beijing on 7 July 1937, between troops of a Chinese army and Japanese units at the Lúgōu Bridge 卢沟桥 (known to the West as the Marco Polo Bridge), made full-scale war a reality. The skirmish marked the beginning of World War II in Asia.

The first part of the war, from July 1937 through February 1939, saw aggressive fighting and many gains by the Japanese. The Japanese armies established control over all of northern and much of eastern China, including Shanghai and all the important coastal cities. Chiang and the Nationalists retreated to Chóngqìng 重庆, Sìchuān Province, with the remnants of his military and civilian government, along with several million others. He made Chongqing his wartime capital.

What happened to the capital Nanjing became a controversial event in Asian history: the Nanjing Massacre, or the Rape of Nanjing (Nánjīng dà túshā 南京大屠杀), a name comprising the war crimes—including murder, rape, the dismembering of human bodies, and the slaughter of domestic and farm animals—perpetrated by Japanese troops during their invasion and occupation of the Nationalist capital from December 1937 to February 1938. After the end of World War II, the Tokyo War Crimes tribunal held the armies of the Japanese general Matsui Iwane responsible for the execution and murder of more than two hundred thousand defenseless and unarmed Chinese soldiers and civilians, and the rape and torture of reportedly twenty thousand women and girls. General Matsui was found guilty by the war tribunal of committing crimes against humanity and was sentenced to death by hanging.

Although the massacre was well reported at the time, for years afterward the Japanese government refused to admit to the crimes, and the Chinese government failed to raise the issue internationally. In the 1980s the Chinese began a serious study of the massacre, revealing that as many as three hundred thousand lives may have actually been lost. Some members of the nationalist movement in Japan have, ever since World War II, tried to discredit evidence of the massacre, while some in China have sought to confirm and even exaggerate any findings with the intent of convincing Asians that Japan's ultra rightists were—and still are—a threat to world peace. No matter what the exact scope of this horrific event, at the onset of World War II on the

Japanese soldiers lower
Chinese prisoners into a pit
before burying them alive.

European front the Nanjing Massacre turned the sympathies of the rest of the world even more toward China and away from the Japanese aggressors.

The Attrition Phase (Xiāohào jiēduàn 消耗阶段)

The attrition phase of the war with Japan began in March 1939. In theory, the Communists and the Nationalists had been cooperating in the struggle against the Japanese since the end of 1936. In reality, though, they operated separately and with different tactics. The Nationalists emphasized building their strength with U.S. assistance beyond the reach of the Japanese forces, while the Communists looked for little or no outside assistance and counted on mobilizing the Chinese people to resist the Japanese through guerrilla warfare. The Nationalists and Communists, of course, shared an ultimate goal: each hoped the conflict with Japan would damage the other side more; each hoped to be standing at the end to finally take the prize—the right to rule China.

In March 1940, a disgruntled Nationalist leader, Wāng Jīngwèi 汪精卫, established a government under Japanese control at Nanjing that ruled over Japanese-occupied China. He died in 1944 before the end of the war, but he, his close associates, and his wife were all tried for treason following Japan's surrender.

Before 1940, Nationalist China had received aid from the Soviet Union, which wanted to hold back Japanese expansionism on the Asian mainland. But in late 1940, the Japanese and the Soviets signed a nonaggression pact, and Soviet aid to the Nationalists dissipated. Fortunately for the Nationalists, by 1940 U.S. support for Nationalist China had grown to include significant loans and gifts or low-cost purchases of military goods. Also in 1941, a group of U.S. volunteer pilots under Claire Chennault (known to the Chinese as Chén Nàdé 陈纳德) prepared to go to China to help the Nationalists; they became famous in early 1942 as the Fēihǔduì 飞虎队 (Flying Tigers). This was just the start of years of military cooperation between the United States and the Nationalists.

The long attrition phase of this war lasted five years. Japan's armies were so spread around Asia—particularly after the entry of the U.S. into World War II in December 1941—that they could not undertake serious offensives in China. Seeing U.S. victory over Japan as inevitable, Chiang Kai-shek wanted to hold back his armies from combat so he could defeat the Communists when the war ended—a position that caused conflict with his chief U.S. military adviser, General Joseph Stilwell. The smaller and poorly equipped Communist forces led by Mao worked to perfect their method of protracted guerrilla war against a colonizing power. The Chinese Communist leaders at Yan'an also developed new forms of ideological discipline and methods of working with the common people. This bundle of techniques became known as "The Yan'an Way" (Yán'ān jīngshén 延安精神) and was considered a guiding force for Communist rule right until Mao's death in 1976.

The End of the War with Japan (Kàngzhàn jiéshù 抗战结束)

In April 1944, the Japanese launched their last great offensive in the China war: code-named Ichigo (Number One), it aimed to destroy U.S. airbases in the Nationalist-controlled region near the city of Chángshā 长沙. From these airbases, U.S. long-range bombers were bombing parts of Japan. By early 1945, it was clear that Japanese armies in China were not strong enough for an all-out campaign against the Nationalists and Americans. By the summer of 1945 the war in China ground to a halt, with one exception: as a U.S. invasion of the Japanese home islands seemed imminent, the Soviet Union, under U.S. urging, broke its nonaggression pact with Japan and invaded northeast China. The atomic bombings of Hiroshima and Nagasaki led to the Japanese surrender to the Allies on 15 August 1945. For a time, Japanese troops remained in place around much of China, often assisting the arriving Nationalist armies in establishing their authority.

The war had militarily damaged the Nationalists and gave them a reputation for being undemocratic, corrupt, and inefficient. The overall cost of the war in China was enormous, with perhaps 18 million Chinese dead. China's economic system also lay in ruins, partly as a result of inflation of more than 200 percent a year between 1942 and 1945. Chiang Kai-shek raced to establish the authority of his Nationalist government throughout China, even in those areas of the country where the Nationalists hadn't been in control prior to 1937. The Chinese Communists were confident that their "Yan'an Way" could lead to a successful nationwide revolutionary movement, and they prepared to struggle with the Nationalists once more.

The Civil War Begins (Nèizhàn bàofā 内战爆发)

The different tactics the Nationalists and Communists used to fight Japan basically determined which side won when they fought each other in a civil war. From 1941 through 1945 the Nationalist government held back from major offensives against the Japanese while acquiring a powerful and generous ally in the United States. At the same time, the Nationalists suffered from serious economic problems and from weakening popular support. The Communists under Mao made "simple living and self-reliance" (jiān-kǔ-pǔ-sù 艰苦朴素, zì-lì-gēng-shēng 自力更生) into a patriotic virtue; they were admired for their aggressive anti-Japanese nationalism and, with the memory of warlordism fresh in the minds of the Nationalists, because they were not corrupt. Most important, the Communists under Mao increased their territorial control across northern China, knitting together popular regional governments behind Japanese lines. Even with little outside support, the Communist forces grew tremendously in numbers and in confidence.

Topics for Further Study

Black Gold Politics

Civil War 1945–1949

People's Liberation Army

World War II in Asia

After Japan's collapse in August 1945, Chiang rushed his forces to major cities all over China, typically using U.S. air and naval units to transport his armies and demanding that defeated Japanese units hand control over to his forces. (It is reputed that Chiang, in relief at the war's end, celebrated Japan's defeat by playing a recording of "Ave Maria" on the gramophone.) The Nationalists wound up with military and political strength throughout China, but it was thinly spread. The Communist strategy was to build on the strength they had in northern China. In a bold move, Mao Zedong dispatched General Lín Biāo 林彪 (1908–1971) with a large army to northeast China, hoping the occupying Soviet forces might aid their fellow Communists. Lin Biao's forces received some assistance from the Soviet armies, primarily by letting Japanese arms fall into Soviet hands. The Soviet Union still recognized Chiang's Nationalist government and accepted the Nationalist occupation of the region's cities, ports, and railway.

Chiang and the Nationalists hoped for massive U.S. intervention on their behalf in the conflict. The United States continued to give extensive military support to the Nationalists, but as World War II had just concluded, President Truman believed the U.S. Congress and the American people wouldn't agree to the amounts of money, materiel, and fighting men needed to ensure a Chinese Nationalist victory. American efforts in 1945 and 1946 to forge a compromise between the Nationalists and the Communists were also unsuccessful.

Overall, Nationalist armies fared well in these early battles. By late 1946 Chiang was certain of victory, and he reorganized his government with a new constitution, followed by national elections. In March 1947, the Nationalists captured the Communist wartime capital of Yan'an, making them even more confident.

Turning of the Tide (Xíngshì dà nìzhuǎn 形势大逆转)

The Nationalist cause then began to sputter. Wartime inflation deepened, making it difficult to restart the economy. In the summer and fall of 1947, Communist armies began to win victories in northern China. Over the following months, Lin Biao's

Thought Experiment

Mainland China and the island of Taiwan have been separate political entities since 1949. How do they (and the reasons for their split) compare to the Union and the Confederacy in the U.S. Civil War?

Communist forces won a series of major battles in northeast China, overtaking the region by November 1948 after destroying many of the Nationalists' best armies. Instead of relying on guerrilla warfare, the Communist military moved in regular battlefield formations: large infantry armies supported by some tanks, artillery, and aircraft. Nationalist divisions began to surrender to the Communists, later reappearing to fight on the Communist side with their modern American equipment.

In October 1948 the.Communists opened a general offensive in southern Shandong and northern Jiangsu known as the Huaihai Campaign (Huáihǎi zhànyì 淮海战役). Chiang threw his best remaining divisions into the fight only to lose them by January 1949. As the steady losses became evident, the Nationalist general in command of the Beijing-Tianjin region surrendered with two hundred thousand soldiers. Opposition elements within the Nationalist Party forced Chiang to resign in January 1949, and General Lǐ Zōngrén 李宗仁 became acting president. In April 1949, Communist armies crossed the Yángzǐ (Chang) River and began mopping up the last areas of Nationalist resistance.

At the outset of the war with Japan in 1937, Chiang and his followers had retreated from Nanjing to Chongqing. This time, in late 1949, Chiang and about two million Nationalists fled across the Strait of Táiwān claiming the mandate of the Republic of China and hoping for a comeback to recover the mainland. The relationship between the victorious Chinese Communists and the Chinese Nationalists has thawed significantly today, but in fact the civil war has never formally ended.

Why did the Nationalists lose? At the time, some said their defeat was the result of not enough support from the United States. This led some Americans to the finger-pointing question of "Who lost China?" The inflation and near economic collapse in China during that period certainly didn't help the Nationalist cause. The Chinese

Communists also probably had better generals with a better military strategy. A major reason for the triumph of Mao and the Communists may have to do with Mao's continuing premise about revolution: win the support of a large number of the people, particularly in the countryside, to ensure success. This was something the Nationalists, with their old-style bureaucratic power and significant international support, were never able to do.

Communists in Power: The Early Years

(Gòngchǎndǎng Zhízhèng Zǎoqī
共产党执政早期:)
1949–1966

*T*he new era of Communist rule under the People's Republic of China (PRC) began on 1 October 1949, when Mao Zedong, perched at the top of the Tiananmen gateway to the old Imperial Palace, proclaimed: "China has stood up." For the PRC this date is equivalent to the July 4th holiday in the United States, and is known by the Chinese as National Day.

One of the first tasks of the new government ruling China was to determine what areas China should include. The three northeastern-most provinces in China (Hēilóngjiāng, Jílín, and Liáoníng) were fully integrated into the country. So were autonomous areas, the places where many Chinese minority groups lived. Inner Mongolia Autonomous Region (Nei Menggu [Mongol] 内蒙古) had already been formally established in 1947. Other minority areas, such as Xīnjiāng Uygur, a large and remote western region; Níngxiǎ Huí, to its east; Guǎngxī Zhuàng, in southern China along the Vietnam border; and Tibet, which had claimed to rule itself since 1913, became part of China but were not deemed official Autonomous Regions until the 1950s and 1960s.

Then there was the island of Taiwan, where Chiang Kai-shek and his Nationalist followers intended to reestablish the Republic of China. In October 1949, a Communist force tried to seize the small island of Jīnmén 金门 in the Taiwan Strait about five miles off the mainland coast. The Red Army, now called by its new name, Rénmín jiěfàngjūn 人民解放军 (People's Liberation Army or PLA), failed to capture the island, which showed how tough a job it would be to invade the much larger island of Taiwan. So the "liberation" of Taiwan was indefinitely postponed. Despite their refusal to give up using force, the PRC adopted a new policy of "peaceful reunification" based on increased economic, social, and cultural exchanges that, they hoped, would lead to political reconciliation.

A second task for the new People's Republic was to see where it fit into the postwar world order. At the beginning of the Cold War, choosing sides seemed to be necessary. In December 1949, Mao left China for the first time in his life and went to Moscow to meet with his Soviet counterpart, Joseph Stalin. The result was the Sino-Soviet Treaty of Alliance and Mutual Assistance. One important provision was a promise that China and the Soviet Union would support each other if either was attacked by Japan.

War did break out in June 1950 between North and South Korea. After North Korean troops had overrun much of the south, United Nations forces (led by U.S. troops) had pushed the North Koreans back to within 50 miles of the North Korea's border with China. Fearing a close U.S. presence, the PRC sent massive "voluntary" armed forces (zhìyuàn jūn 志愿军) into the war, driving back the United Nations forces to the 38th parallel—the boundary between North and South Korea where everything had started. A stalemate finally ended in a truce agreement that was signed in June 1953. The war affected China in a number of ways, besides the more than seven hundred thousand Chinese casualties, among them Mao Zedong's son. The threat of war was used to bolster support for the PRC, and the rift between the Chinese Communists and the United States grew wider. One domestic campaign the PRC promoted during the war was called Kàng Měi-yuán-Cháo 抗美援朝 (Resist America, Aid [North] Korea). During and after the war, the United States threw greater support to Chiang Kai-shek's government in Taiwan.

Reforms and Campaigns (Biàngé yǔ yùndòng 变革与运动)

In the first few years after the PRC was founded, a number of reforms significantly transformed China. The Agrarian Reform Law (Tǔ gǎi fǎ 土改法) of 1950 was part of a program that confiscated and redistributed much of China's cultivated land. The Marriage Law (Hūnyīn fǎ 婚姻法) in the same year replaced the "feudal" marriage system with the New Democratic system, where women were allowed to choose their spouses freely and were given equal rights in divorce, child custody, and property. (Even so, in rural areas many traditional features of marriage, based on Confucian ideals of filial piety, survived.) Educational opportunities were extended to many more people; by 1952 about 60 percent of students who were age-eligible for elementary education attended school, a big increase from earlier eras.

Soon the CCP gave up its more moderate attitude about change and reconstruction and instead started to launch radical political campaigns intended to reinforce party control. First was the Three-Anti Campaign (Sān fǎn yùndòng 三反运动) against corruption, waste, and bureaucratism, with government and industry employees as its targets. The Five-Anti Campaign (Wǔ fǎn yùndòng 五反运动), to combat bribery, tax evasion, theft of state assets, cheating on government contracts, and stealing capital, followed. This campaign targeted the Chinese capitalists. A hidden agenda of the Five-Anti Campaign was to seize factories and property from blacklisted capitalists and place them under government control. The total number of people who perished in these campaigns may have been in the hundreds of thousands.

In May 1956, Mao announced that the Communist government would relax its strict control over freedom of thought and expression. This new program soon adopted the slogan of "Let a hundred flowers bloom and a hundred thoughts contend" (bǎi-huā-qí-fàng, bǎi-jiā-zhēng-míng 百花齐放、百家争鸣), an invitation for intellectuals to voice criticisms of party leaders and government policies. (The phrase "a hundred schools of thought" reverberates throughout China's history in reference to the myriad philosophies, from Confucianism to Daoism to Legalism and more, that proliferated during the Warring States period 475–221 BCE.) Other more open policies, such as greater access to foreign publications, were promoted in an attempt to win over intellectuals disillusioned with many of the changes in China since 1949.

Mao and other leaders of the CCP were shocked by the intense criticism growing up as a result of his Hundred Flowers campaign. Expecting to get ideas about how things could be done better by the government, they were surprised to hear that many Chinese felt a different government itself might be better. By July 1957, the party

Thought Experiment

One political party runs the Chinese government. If your government was suddenly limited to one political party, and you were opposed to its actions and policies, how would you go about affecting change?

launched a new campaign to repudiate those who had taken up Mao's offer to give criticism, and about a half to three-quarters of a million intellectuals, including Zhū Róngjī 朱镕基, who later became premier of the PRC from 1998 to 2003, were denounced as "Rightists" (Yòupài 右派). Many were persecuted and others sent to the countryside to "rectify their thinking through labor." It was only in 1979, three years after the death of Mao, that these denounced intellectuals had their good names restored in the eyes of the Chinese Communist Party, a process called rehabilitation, when some of the excesses of the period were finally admitted.

The Great Leap Forward (Dàyuèjìn 大跃进)

In 1958 Mao launched a new program called the Great Leap Forward (Dàyuèjìn 大跃进). The goal, in Mao's vision, was to develop and modernize China in order to catch up to and surpass Great Britain and the United States. Throughout the 1950s, China had been following a development strategy similar to that of the Soviet Union, giving priority to heavy industry. Disappointed with the results, Mao and his fellow leaders believed that through massive social mobilization China could simultaneously develop both industry and agriculture.

Mao had all along sought to promote large collectives and communes, believing that larger groups could be more efficient economically and better positioned to promote social equality. Mao demanded even larger collectives be formed as part of the Great Leap Forward program.

Earlier political campaigns had hushed any dissenting views. By now, whenever Mao spoke in favor of something, those who wanted to succeed in China raced to agree with his views as quickly and loudly as possible. Within two months in 1958, most provinces claimed a successful transition to People's Communes (Rénmín gōngshè 人民公社) totaling 26,500, each averaging about 4,800 households. The communes abolished private property and, along with it, any personal economic incentive for farmers to increase their productivity. To allow women to join the work force, commune members were encouraged to abandon their own kitchens and dine in communal mess halls.

In the middle of this euphoric transition to collectivization, Mao stopped paying attention to reality. The state statistical system stopped functioning rationally, and officials made wild claims of bountiful harvests. With imaginary abundance, the share of grain the state took to sell for export was sharply increased—in part to speed up paying off the debt China owed to the Soviet Union. Relations between the two Communist states had worsened.

By spring 1959, many communes had exhausted their grain reserves, and China was afflicted by famine. During the Lushan Conference 庐山会议 of 1959, Mao unleashed a "second leap" and pushed again for communal mess halls. The situation worsened. The toll, caused more by politics than nature, was staggering. China's mortality rates rose from 12 per 1,000 in 1958 to 25.4 per 1,000 in 1960, a year in which China's net population dropped by 10 million people. One demographic estimate attributes the number of excess deaths in China, during the years from 1958 to 1961, to between 15 and 30 million. This was by far the worst famine in human history.

The Great Leap shattered people's belief in large rural organizations and government policies. It prompted Mao and his colleagues to scale down the size of communes. Popular support for communes dwindled because of the famine, laying the foundation for China's eventual decollectivization following Mao's death. Ironically, instead of accelerating China's march toward Communism, the Great Leap eventually helped China to embrace market economy, China's euphemism for capitalism.

The immediate effect of the disaster, however, was that Mao became largely withdrawn from day-to-day control of China's affairs in the early 1960s. Already in April 1959, Mao's former position of Chairman of the People's Republic had been taken by his political rival Liú Shàoqí 刘少奇, who had questioned Mao's policies along with Dèng Xiǎopíng 邓小平 (the CCP's general secretary), and economic strategist Chén Yún 陈云. Still representing Mao's views was Minister of Defense Lin Biao 林彪 and Mao's wife Jiāng Qīng 江青. All of these people would become major players in the political drama that began in 1966.

The Cultural Revolution

(Wénhuà gémìng文化革命)
1966–1976

*T*he largest and most significant of the ideological campaigns launched by Mao Zedong was the Great Proletarian Cultural Revolution (*Wúchǎnjiējí wénhuà dà gémìng* 无产阶级文化大革命), or simply the Cultural Revolution

(*Wénhuà gémìng* 文化革命). This mass movement involving many millions of people, marked by violence and even some localized civil wars, helped to create a cult around Mao, despite the setbacks in power he would endure. According to Mao and his followers, the Cultural Revolution (CR, 1966–1976) was a continuation of the struggle waged by the working class against the oppressive capitalists and their supporters, labeled the "bourgeoisie."

Permanent Revolution (Yǒngyuǎn gémìng 永远革命)

In the mid-1960s, as chairman of CCP, the humiliated Mao still commanded great power and influence. He resented the moderate economic policies implemented by his former comrades in the CCP leadership after the failure of his own radical Great Leap Forward. He claimed that CCP was beginning to act like a new ruling class and that its growing elitism could end up in a "capitalist restoration." The Cultural Revolution was thus both an ideological campaign to prevent this alleged return to capitalism and a struggle for power with more moderate elements of the CCP.

Mao believed that China's economy and society needed to become increasingly more socialized. He was for a campaign-style of politics that mobilized the masses, and his theory was that China required a state of "permanent revolution." Liu, on the other hand, was in favor of careful economic planning under the control of the CCP. He reintroduced measures, such as rural markets and private farm plots for the peasants, to encourage production by offering material incentives to the Chinese people.

To face his opponents, Mao turned to China's students and to the People's Liberation Army for support. Mao chose the mayor of Beijing, Péng Zhēn 彭真 (1902–1997), to lead the new movement and initially allowed Peng to do so in his own way. After Peng tried to limit the Cultural Revolution's scope strictly to cultural affairs, Mao had Peng purged—the term *purge* took on an especially ominous tone during these ten years—and established a Cultural Revolution Group under the control of Jiang Qing and Chén Bódá 陈伯达, who both encouraged and directed much of the radical activities of the next several years.

The Red Guard (Hóngwèibīng 红卫兵)

In May 1966, an organization of high school and university students called the Red Guard (*Hóngwèibīng* 红卫兵) formed in Beijing, in part as a protest to a play, written by the historian Wú Hán 吴晗, called *Hǎi Ruì bà guān* 海瑞罢官 (*Dismissed from Office*). In that play, a Míng dynasty official is removed from power for objecting to the emperor's confiscation of land from peasants. The performance was seen as an attack on Mao's own policies, and Red Guards made it their cause to be Mao's personal protectors and soldiers in the socialist revolution. They began creating slogans and staging demonstrations critical of their teachers and schools. Mao gave his blessing to the Red Guards by writing them a letter that praised their activities. During late 1966, Mao attended six gigantic rallies in Beijing in which a total of more than

Topics for Further Study

Famine

Revolutions

Little Red Book (Quotations from Chairman Mao Zedong)

10 million Red Guards participated. The organization quickly spread throughout the country.

The first official party document on the Cultural Revolution was the decision adopted by a plenum of the Central Committee in August 1966. It declared the CR to be a new stage in China's revolution and emphasized the need to struggle against and overthrow those in authority taking the capitalist road. The decision endorsed the battle in education against so-called bourgeois academic authorities, but it warned against violence as a means of resolving differences. It held that the "great majority" of cadres—party administrators and professionals—were "good" or "comparatively good," and suggested that Red Guards should not attack them without good reason. But as the Red Guard grew in number and fervor, its members frequently disregarded the party's admonishments.

In keeping with Mao's campaign to destroy the "four olds" (*sìjiù* 四旧)—old thought, old culture, old customs, and old practices—the Red Guard mobilized to aggressively reject traditional culture. At first their activities seemed harmless enough, like renaming streets, for example. (Some Red Guards attempted to change traffic patterns, thinking that the color red, as the symbol of the Chinese revolution, should signify "go.") They shunned anything foreign, including fashion and hairstyles. As the campaign grew more violent, Red Guards began torturing and killing people with "bad class backgrounds," destroying stores selling luxury goods, burning theater and opera props, smashing Confucian tombstones, and ransacking archaeological and religious sites. Only direct action by the Central Committee kept Red Guards from storming the Imperial City in Beijing.

In September 1966, when Mao's *Máo zhǔxí yǔlù* (毛主席语录 *Sayings of Chairman Mao Zedong*), was published, the book became an icon for his followers, in particular the Red Guards. By official figures, 350 million copies of this slender volume, commonly referred to as The Little Red Book, had been printed by the end of 1967. Those obsessed with following Mao's thought emphasized class struggle and "serving the people" (the title of Mao's most popular article) rather than oneself or one's family. With all the attacks on "old culture," very few books were published other than those about Mao's philosophy or revolutionary history. Many literary figures were humiliated and even persecuted to death, notably the famous fiction writer and playwright Lǎo Shě (老舍). Traditional theater was banned, and Jiang Qing imposed a theory of "model dramas" (yàngbǎnxì 样板戏), which insisted that all literature and art should reflect the class struggle and promote revolutionary heroism.

Trying to Control the Storm (Shìtú kòngzhì júshì 试图控制局势)

The Red Guards soon splintered into factions, fighting violently as they contested who displayed the most loyalty and commitment. They continued to arrest, torture, and harass anyone seen as a threat to the revolution, including translators, scholars, and military officials. In January 1967, prompted by the Red Guard's continued violence and increased fanaticism, the leaders of the Cultural Revolution commanded the People's Liberation Army to restore order. "Revolutionary Committees" (Géwěihuì 革委会) were then set up in the whole country, from the level of every province down to every factory, school, and people's commune. These committees, which took over the old administrative functions of the government, were considered to be the linchpins of a mass revolutionary movement like the CR. They contained members of the military, the Red Guard (representing the masses), and experienced cadres who had managed to survive the CR to that point. The military, however, soon took the most prominent leadership role in these revolutionary committees.

In the summer of 1967, radical Red Guard activity surged, leading to violent conflict between the Red Guard and the military in several parts of China. The most serious was a three-week civil war in and around Wǔhàn, the capital of Húběi Province. Jiang Qing instigated the conflict, and it ended in a victory for Mao and the Red Guard forces. Disturbances inspired by Red Guards even flared in Hong Kong, and in August they conducted a savage attack on the British chargé d'affaires office in Beijing.

After another period of relative order, fighting broke out again from April to July 1968. Many small-scale civil wars sprang up in southern China, especially in the Guangxi Zhuang Autonomous Region bordering Vietnam. Although Mao believed that "great chaos leads to great order," he moved toward bringing some stability to the country that seemed destined for a wider civil war. On 28 July 1968, Mao, Lin Biao, Jiang Qing, and other leaders interviewed several Red Guard leaders, admonished them, and began sending large numbers of Red Guards to do hard labor in rural areas, a process euphemistically called "receiving re-education from the peasants." In the eyes of the West, these middle- and high-school students became "the rusticated youth of China," but to the peasants and to the young people themselves, they were zhīshi

In 1968, Mao sent Red Guards to the countryside for "re-education," hoping to quash their zealous and violent persecution of those who upheld traditional culture.

qīngnian 知识青年, abbreviated 知青, literally meaning "educated youth." Re-education, also known as *shàng shān xià xiāng* 上山下乡 ("up to the mountains and down to the countryside"), was supposed to give urban youth a broader revolutionary experience, but the CCP's main purpose was to get them out of the cities and cut down on violence. Forcing students and graduates to the countryside may have been Mao's only option to finesse the unsolvable problem of unemployment: the Cultural Revolution had shut down colleges and universities and caused great numbers of factories to close (and jobs to evaporate). What were Chinese youths supposed to do?

Rebuilding the Party (Dǎng de chóngjiàn 党的重建)

In October 1968, a CCP Central Committee plenum condemned Mao's old rival Liu Shaoqi as a traitor and sent him to prison, where the disgraced and battered former Chairman of the PRC was left in absolute solitude to die—of hunger, coldness, trauma, and illness—in the winter of 1969. His death was not even revealed until February 1980 when he was rehabilitated (that is, his reputation was cleared), by the post-Mao

Zhou Enlai 周恩来

Zhou Enlai's (1898–1976) family was native to Shaoxing in Zhejiang Province, known in imperial times for producing well-educated and indispensable aides to high officials. Zhou eventually held high-ranking positions himself, but he also followed his ancestral region's tradition by serving for decades as Mao Zedong's right-hand man.

Zhou's political involvement as a student activist and journalist, in both China and Europe, began during the early years of the May Fourth Movement (1915–1923). After returning to China in 1924, he served as a political commissar in the Whampoa Military Academy, a position that garnered the trust of revolutionary military officers. He was involved in planning the Nanchang Uprising on 1 August 1927, a Communist-led attack retaliating against Chiang Kai-shek's Nationalists.

As one of the founders and leaders of the Red Army, Zhou worked closely with Mao Zedong. After the Long March of 1934–1935 he became Mao's second-in-command, a position he never relinquished. Mao formulated doctrine, while Zhou translated it into practical policies. From the inauguration of the PRC until his death, Zhou was premier of the State Council and a popular figure among the Chinese. As foreign minister from 1949 to 1958, he was respected as a skillful diplomat.

He managed to deflect some blame from Mao for failures such as the Great Leap Forward (1958–1960), and to assuage some damage done by the Cultural Revolution (1966–1976).

The memoirs of Mao's personal physician reveal that Zhou did indeed inherit a proclivity for providing indispensable assistance: he was said to behave obsequiously in Mao's presence, tasting his food to make sure it wasn't poisoned and crawling at Mao's feet like a eunuch serving an emperor. In private, the physician claimed, Mao referred to Zhou dismissively as "his housekeeper." Apparently, the Zhou's servile way was partially a strategy for massaging Mao's ego and easing his paranoia, and partially a relic of feudal tradition and customs.

Although Zhou long suppressed the rivalry between himself and Mao, tensions flared when they both became ill in the mid-1970s. Both sought to leave their stamp on China's future and the direction of the revolution to which they dedicated their lives. Zhou favored Deng Xiaoping, while Mao, thinking of Deng as one who would "go down the capitalist road," preferred the more left-wing Hua Guofeng.

Zhou died on 9 January 1976, exactly nine months before Mao. Mao's credibility had declined because of his extremist policies and his association with the Gang of Four. Zhou's

Zhou Enlai 周恩来 *(Continued)*

reputation, however, soared for his role in rehabilitating persecuted party members. Mao thus prohibited any public outpouring of grief for Zhou. During the Qingming festival for mourning the dead in April 1976, thousands gathered in Tiananmen Square with wreaths, poems, and flowers dedicated to Zhou's memory, and the CCP sent in troops to quash what appeared to be an anti-Mao demonstration. Public morning for Zhou Enlai (Enlai means "coming of grace") was permitted only after Mao's death (and the Gang of Four's arrest) in October.

leadership of Deng Xiaoping. The Ninth Party Congress in April 1969 ended the most radical phase of the Cultural Revolution and stressed the need to unite and work to rebuild the CCP. Appearing as a total victory for Mao, the Party Congress declared Lin Biao his "close comrade-in-arms and successor" and the sole CCP vice chairman.

But challenges to the Cultural Revolution's policies were far from over, especially as the "Lin Biao Affair" began to unfold. Lin mysteriously disappeared in September 1971. According to official accounts that were not released until February 1972, Lin and his main supporters, including his son and wife, had concocted a plot to depose Mao. When the coup was exposed, the official report stated, they fled China to find sanctuary in the Soviet Union, but were killed en route, on 13 September 1971, in a plane crash over Manchuria. The incident raised serious doubts among many Chinese about whether Mao's judgment, in this case his absolute faith in Lin Baio, was as reliable as his near godlike status should demand. The betrayal of this most trusted successor dealt Mao a fatal blow: his health began to fail rapidly, and he never fully recovered.

Around this time enormous changes were taking place in China's foreign relations. After the mostly self-imposed isolation of the earlier part of the Cultural Revolution, China moved to rejoin the international community. In October 1971, China was admitted into the United Nations. In February 1972, President Nixon traveled to China in the hope of reestablishing diplomatic relations, thus recognizing its growing economic and political power. Liaison offices opened in Beijing and Washington D.C. in 1973, and formal diplomatic relations were inaugurated on 1 January 1979. In the first half of the 1970s, China established full diplomatic relations with numerous countries, including several other major Western powers and Japan.

Gang of Four (Sìrén bāng 四人帮)

The Gang of Four is the name given to four influential supporters of the Chinese Cultural Revolution (1966–1976). (It is also the name taken by a British punk rock band of the late 1970s. The Chinese name for the Gang of Four—Siren bang—would be another excellent name for a rock group.)

In 1975 and 1976, when there was much unrest and plotting within the Chinese government, three Politburo members (Zhang Chunqiao, Yao Wenyuan, and Wang Hongwen) along with Jiang Qing, Mao's wife, planned a coup to seize control of China and the Communist Party following Mao's death; Jiang was to succeed Mao as party leader. Mao died on 9 September 1976, and when the gang attempted the takeover, it failed. Early in October all four were arrested and removed from power.

The CCP Central Committee accused them of being "bourgeois careerists, conspirators, and counter-revolutionary double-dealers." In a finger-pointing denunciation in front of thousands in Tiananmen Square on 24 October 1976, Beijing Communist Party leader Wu De was the first to use the term "Gang of Four" in public, blaming them for virtually all the tragic results of the Cultural Revolution. (Although Mao is thought to have coined the term, it had only circulated behind the scenes to identify small cliques isolated from the government.)

The four were accused of treason and other crimes, especially the persecution of large numbers of people including CCP and state leaders. During the trial by a special court in 1980, Jiang Qing argued she was simply carrying out Mao's wishes—it's true that none of them could have acted as they did without Mao's support—but all four were convicted.

The Chinese government went to considerable lengths to clear Mao of any criminal motivation or action for a decade's worth of devastation; clearly the gang was meant to take the fall. Since the 1980s the official history of the Chinese Communist Party states that 6 October 1976, the day of the gang's arrest, marks the end of the Cultural Revolution. There is, as of 2009, no openly available Chinese-language account of the period, although one appeared in the 1980s but was quickly banned. The Cultural Revolution remains a sensitive topic in China even today—symbolizing for some a period of darkness and suffering; for others, as Mao's popularity soared, the first time China had experienced anything like mass religious fervor; and for others still a time of liberation.

Struggles within the CCP leadership continued, but a more relaxed atmosphere prevailed. Deng Xiaoping was again referred to in the press as vice premier in April 1973, after seven years in disgrace. In August 1973, Premier Zhou Enlai replaced Lin Biao as Mao's first deputy and CCP vice chairman. To counterbalance Zhou's influence, Mao handpicked for his own successor Wáng Hóngwén 王洪文, a radical young worker from Shanghai. To keep the influence of the Cultural Revolution alive, Mao encouraged his radical supporters to initiate a series of ideological campaigns, some insidiously directed at Zhou Enlai, a supporter of Deng Xiaoping. When (for the first time) millions of Beijing students and citizens expressed their anger at the policies of Mao and his supporters by mourning Zhou's death on Tiananmen Square in January 1976, they were suppressed as counter-revolutionaries. Deng Xiaoping was blamed for instigating the mass protest and removed again from his leadership positions.

Mao Zedong died in September 1976. Four of the most influential supporters of the Cultural Revolution—Zhāng Chūnqiáo 张春桥, Yáo Wényuán 姚文元, Wang Hongwen, and Jiang Qing (Mao's wife), infamously known as the Gang of Four (Sìrén bāng 四人帮)—then staged a coup to seize control of the CCP and install Jiang as its leader. In October the Gang was arrested, signaling the end of the Cultural Revolution an era that most agree had harmed millions of people and set back China's development for years. (See the sidebar about the Gang.)

China After Mao

(Máo shēn hòu de Zhōngguó
毛身后的中国)
1976–present

As the People's Republic of China moved from the era dominated by Mao Zedong to the one that followed, key words like "ideological," "revolution," and "violence" gave way to "pragmatism," "modernization," and "rapid growth." In some basic ways—such as the dominant role of the Chinese Communist Party and the limits placed on political freedom—China continued to resemble the country that Mao ruled. In other ways, it became very different, with more change every year. Here we take a quick tour through the most notable political developments of the last three decades.

Judging the Past (Píngpàn guòqù 评判过去)

Trusting neither the radicals led by the Gang of Four nor the moderates headed by Zhou Enlai and Deng Xiaoping in the CCP, Mao had handpicked Huà Guófēng 华国锋 (1921–2008), a political dark horse, as his successor. A Mao loyalist, Hua led post-Mao China only briefly, and yet he was instrumental in the capture of the Gang of Four and others blamed for the Cultural Revolution. In 1978, Hú Yàobāng 胡耀邦 (1915–1989) replaced Hua as the CCP chair and Zhào Zǐyáng 赵紫阳 (1919–2005) as China's premier. However, it was the chairman of the Central Military Commission and vice premier of the state, Deng Xiaoping, who came to wield the most power.

From late 1978 onward, Deng was able to dictate an economic policy that went against Mao's in just about every way. Deng's regime first acknowledged some of the errors of the past. Among the many people who had been wrongly judged by the previous Communist regimes—and thus were deemed worthy to be rehabilitated, or welcomed back to society with their reputations intact—were millions of landowners and rich peasants during the early 1950s; five hundred thousand or more "Rightists" during the late 1950s; several million "antisocialists" during the early 1960s; and at least 3 million denounced (or worse) during the Cultural Revolution. Many of these rehabilitations were posthumous. The entire campaign to fix past mistakes was pursued for about five years.

What would be said about Mao, the founding father and the powerful leader, concerning his involvement in those periods of historic misjudgment and tragedy? Mao's tomb is still the major visitor attraction at Tiananmen Square, and his portrait is the centerpiece of the gate to the Forbidden City, from which point he seems to survey the entire expanses of the Square. Some compare his portrait, still seen all over China, to that of the Buddha in its ubiquity and confident serenity. The answer, for the majority in China at least, was to treat him like a split personality of sorts: "good Mao" versus "bad Mao." The earlier Mao (maybe 70 percent of his rule) and his basic ideas were said to be good, while the later 30 percent was open for criticism. For example, a 1981 resolution by the Central Committee of CCP on "questions of party history" called the Cultural Revolution a complete disaster, and said that Mao and even the Central Committee were "partly responsible" for allowing it to happen.

Mao's portrait, as ubiquitous in China as images of the Buddha, presides over Tiananmen Square, where his body lies in state.

The Four Modernizations
(Sì ge xiàndàihuà 四个现代化)

After an historical era where devotion to Communist ideology (or to Mao) were the requirements for success or even survival in China, a more practical attitude took over. Maoist slogans had included "Politics in command" and "Red over expert." In other words, it was better to be correct politically than simply correct. Now there was a return to a different, more traditional Chinese slogan for ruling a state: *shí-shì-qiú-shì* 实事求是 ("seek truth from facts").

Deng's program for moving China forward was called the Four Modernizations (Sì ge xiàndàihuà 四个现代化). The goal was for China to progress in agriculture, industry, science and technology, and defense. The new leaders began rebuilding support among non-Communist classes, especially the former downtrodden intellectuals, business people, and those with overseas connections.

China's leaders were determined that China would change economically and militarily but not much politically. In March 1979 Deng issued the Four Cardinal Principles (Sì xiàng jīběn yuánzé 四项基本原则): China must follow (1) the socialist path, (2) the dictatorship of the proletariat, (3) the leadership of CCP, and (4) Marxism-Leninism-Mao Zedong Thought (a special Russian/Chinese blend of communist and socialist doctrines). Like any dynasty, the CCP was determined to continue its monopoly of power.

How did the Four Modernizations work? First, the "production responsibility system" improved the agricultural situation. As opposed to Mao's communes, production teams of twenty-five to forty families were contracted to produce a certain amount on allotted parcels of land. Individual farms were able to keep more if they produced more through side enterprises such as selling pigs and chickens. During the Cultural Revolution, farmers had only been allowed to produce the grain they were told to grow, and enterprises involving monetary transactions were considered "incipient capitalism." Now a whole community could plan together to maximize production and income; they had an incentive. The state also increased produce prices and allowed the revival of private markets. The resulting increase in both national and individual production was a triumph for Deng's initial reforms.

In industrial development, Deng's major break with the past was opening up to foreign trade, technology, and investment. Earlier policies in the PRC had stressed self-sufficiency and a Soviet-style economy where the direction came from the top. Beginning in the 1980s, there was a new emphasis on local initiative and the production of consumer goods for foreign export. A side effect of this was the explosive growth of those coastal areas that had traditionally been involved in foreign trade.

In 1980, Special Economic Zones (Jīngjì tèqū 经济特区) were established in the south, such as Shēnzhèn 深圳 next to Hong Kong, where joint ventures between foreign companies and state-owned enterprises were encouraged. International trade requires reliable contract law, so new law codes were published and law school programs revived. In the other areas of the Four Modernizations, Chinese work in science and technology was allowed to recover from the restrictions imposed by Mao's anti-intellectualism. The People's Liberation Army also worked to modernize itself.

Over all, the economic reform pushed by Deng Xiaoping and other party leaders in the 1980s had many successes. From 1979 to 2009, the growth in China's GDP (gross domestic product) averaged more than nine percent per year. How much did the Chinese people benefit from this progress? A good deal by some estimates, 400 million people have been lifted out of poverty in the past forty years. But when assessing economic growth in a country such as China it's important to factor in population growth. China's population passed 600 million in the mid-1950s, was 820 million by 1970, topped one billion in the early 1980s, and reached more than 1.33 billion in 2009.

Even with improved agricultural policies and red-hot economic development, it was difficult to keep up. With increased manufacturing production, the gap between the conditions in the country and the cities grew. In 1979, the "one-child family" (*dúshēngzǐ* 独生子) policy was introduced, primarily for urban residents: couples that did not agree to have only one child could lose part of their income and other benefits from the state. Although this policy significantly slowed the rate of population growth—so much so that China's population is predicted to fall below India's by 2025—its wisdom is in question as China, in the twenty-first century, worries about a shrinking workforce, an aging population, a striking gender imbalance, and the emotional ramifications of abortion. In July 2009, the city of Shanghai, one of China's largest (population 20 million) began to confront these issues, offering counseling and actively encouraging eligible young couples to have a second child.

Calls for Political Change (Hūyù zhèngzhì biàngé 呼吁政治变革)

In October 1978, activists began to post "big character" posters discussing politics on a brick wall in Beijing (the Democracy Wall, *mínzhǔ qiáng* 民主墙). This was the start of what became known as the Democracy Wall Movement. A leading member was an electrician named Wèi Jīngshēng 魏京生, who advocated democracy as a "fifth modernization." Deng Xiaoping at first regarded those in the Democracy Wall Movement as allies against surviving Maoists and gave them a measure of support. Deng and his allies also had their own ideas for changing China's political system, though in a limited and controlled way. For example, Deng blamed feudal and undemocratic traditions in China for the recent overconcentration of power in one person (meaning Mao, of course), which had resulted in excesses like the Cultural Revolution. Deng advocated that the roles and powers of the CCP and the Chinese government be separated, and he called for more participation of the people and debate in the party itself. He even allowed discussions about direct elections at all levels and a two-house national parliament so long as the CCP would maintain overall power.

Supporters of the Democracy Wall Movement wanted an even wider debate on how China should be governed, and this turned out to be too much for the leaders of the CCP. As a warning to others, the human rights activist Wei Jingsheng was arrested in April 1979 and sentenced to fifteen years in prison. Chinese intellectuals and the students they taught remained disillusioned. The rise of Poland's Solidarity trade union movement around that time (led by Lech Walesa, who had been, coincidentally, an electrician like Wei Jingsheng), demonstrated the danger of relaxing controls over mass movements.

牧师 的 空 饼 木

方达手

（！你们闭上眼睛
把我把你们送进
主义天堂。

你们吃是菜的 药物
绒鲁.药方药的.买
了受药物.你们现在比
猪人 双套的死多了.

扫方针灸！

This caricature of Madame Mao was posted on the Democracy Wall, initially supported in 1978 by the government to criticize past leaders and failed government programs; the wall was shut down in 1979 when people began to target current leadership and government. PHOTO BY JOAN LEBOLD COHEN.

With a lack of political reform, the changes created by economic reform created major dilemmas for the CCP. China was on its way to becoming a major economic power, but only after giving up many tenets of its original ideology and retreating from full socialist ownership to mixed ownership and markets. In 1987, Zhao Ziyang (who was then the general secretary of the CCP) declared that China was still in the initial stage of socialism and that full socialism could be achieved only when all methods of industrial production were fully developed and modernized.

By the late 1980s, Zhao was promoting some modest proposals to build a socialist democracy, such as a broadening of representation and participation in the political system by new groups and experts in particular areas, and by developing the national and lower-level People's Congresses. Beginning in 1986, university students began to call for more freedom of speech and a greater role in choosing officials.

Hu Yaobang, a former leader of the CCP popularly thought to be a supporter of democracy, died in April 1989. Beijing students held demonstrations in his memory. The seventieth anniversary of 4 May 1919, the date of the demonstration that gave the May Fourth Movement it name, was also marked by unofficial parades. Student demonstrators began camping out on Beijing's Tiananmen Square, where workers, intellectuals, and out-of-towners eventually joined by them. The party leadership was unsure what to do. On the night of 3 June, army units opened fire on demonstrators in the streets and on the square, and hundreds were killed.

The repercussions from the Tiananmen Square incident were great. The Chinese government arrested many people suspected of being part of the pro-democracy movement, and hopes for political reform died. The rest of the world was shocked by the brutal suppression of a peaceful protest. Zhao Ziyang was relieved from power for not doing enough to control the situation; and Deng Xiaoping gradually gave up his important posts in the party and government, though he remained highly influential until his death in 1997. Deng was the last link with the early years of the CCP. An era ended, but the political leadership he had approved stayed in place, and economic modernization moved forward.

The Third and Fourth Generations (Dì sān dài hé dì sì dài lǐngdǎo 第三代和第四代领导)

In the 1990s, leadership in China passed to what was known as the "third generation" of Chinese Communists—the first being Mao and his colleagues from before the founding of the PRC in 1949, and the second those from the early days of Communist rule with Deng Xiaoping at its core. The significant posts passed on to Jiāng Zémín 江泽民 (b. 1926) in what seemed to be the first orderly succession of leadership in CCP history. Jiang endorsed Deng Xiaoping's Four Cardinal Principles. The collapse of Soviet and Eastern European Communism in the late 1980s had shown that the Marxist-Leninist part of the controlling ideology didn't seem to be on the winning side of history. After the unsuccessful moves in the 1980s for greater democracy in China, most Chinese had few hopes for changes politically and ideologically, and they turned their attention to more practical matters.

Jiang's period of rule saw continued economic development, and such events as the transfer of power in Hong Kong (from Great Britain to the PRC) in 1997 and in Macao (from Portugal to the PRC) in 1999. In 2000 Jiang Zemin announced his Three Represents (Sān ge dàibiǎo 三个代表) theory, which held that the party had always represented the most advanced productive forces, most advanced culture, and the basic interests of the Chinese masses. The 1990s in China had been marked, though, by rising corruption in many areas and growing environmental pollution from unchecked development. Experiments with a market economy also resulted in rapidly rising costs in education and health care.

Hú Jǐntāo 胡锦涛 (b. 1942) became President in November 2001. Over the next few years, Hu took on all of the important posts in the party and government, just as Jiang had before him. Fifteen years younger than Jiang, Hu was a representative of the fourth generation of leaders, those too young to have been active politically in the early days of the PRC. This generation is known for a more technocratic approach to problems—though with the same insistence on the premier place of the CCP that its predecessors had.

China entered the World Trade Organization in 2001. The event marked a milestone in China's progress: a country whose economy had once been hamstrung by government control was on its way to becoming one of the world's great economic powers. The booming Chinese economy continues to grow, while corruption, environmental problems, and limited political freedom continue as well. The selection of Beijing as the site for the 2008 Olympic Games and Shanghai as the site for the 2010 World Expo confirmed the greater role China now plays on the world stage. The spotlight will continue to shine on China as it faces problems and challenges in the years ahead.

Chapter 4:
China Today

Zhōngguó nǐ bì zhī 中国你必知

*N*ot long ago China stunned the world with the opening ceremony of the 2008 Olympic Games in Beijing. Who can forget the cast of thousands—women, men, and children—in perfect synchronization? Or the American commentators gamely trying to speak a few words of Chinese? Or the criticisms of China that continued to bubble up, though not so intensely as during the torch relay in the spring?

In 2009, the People's Republic of China celebrated its sixtieth birthday with another extravagant (but more inward-looking) display. In the days since then, at international financial summits and at the U.N. Climate Conference in Copenhagen in December 2009, China has done what everyone agreed it aimed to do by making (and winning) its Olympic bid—China stepped onto the world stage as a great power (and, according to some, *the* great power) of the twenty-first century.

Wide-ranging issues—from climate change and pandemics to terrorism and global economic integration—face all nations of the world today. China's role in shaping policies to address these challenges is now undeniable. Many see this prime position as a reason for anxiety—China's size and one-party government structure make it a giant that can act decisively and independently—and some view China as an outright threat. Others see China's positive attributes—its focus on family and education; its traditional reluctance to use force or invasion (except of course in situations where it considers a territory an essential part of China, like Tibet or Taiwan); its work ethic, resourcefulness, and resilience; and its responsiveness to new challenges as seen in today's rapid development and implementation of renewable energy technologies—as holding promise for the world at large. The revival of Confucianism in China, for instance, is an indication of China's ongoing self-examination. In the late 1980s Chinese culture was viewed as "backward," an impediment to modernity. China's economic might in the twenty-first century has brought about renewed cultural pride, and

---

Topics for Further Study

Perspectives on China—Western

Reforms since 1978–1979

Taiwan Strait (Cross-Strait
    Relations)

Communism, once a source of inspiration and impetus for change, has lost much of its old appeal. Instead many Chinese—government officials, intellectuals, and ordinary citizens alike—seek guidance from Confucian tradition. Based on the principles that the good in life stems from embracing socially responsible relationships and political commitment, Confucian ethics can, many believe, fill the moral vacuum that often accompanies modernization in both Eastern and Western societies.

Debates about whether China's position as a superpower is "good" or "bad" will continue, of course, and events in the news will be used to support widely disparate points of view. China gets a great deal of attention in U.S. and other Western media, but experts tell us that many topics are blown out of proportion and treated without sufficient context. Some issues create tensions between nations, businesses, and individuals. (We know, for example, one happily married couple, Chinese and American, who simply cannot discuss Tibet because their perspectives are so different.) Because China changes so quickly, a book like this cannot compete with sources that offer breaking news about the latest developments in China, nor can it provide comprehensive coverage about global challenges urgently requiring Sino-American and international cooperation. But *This Is China*, and especially this section, *can* help you read between the lines of "China stories" in the news.

We have compiled here several short overviews about concepts, issues, and topics that are fundamental to understanding China (and the country's collective psyche) in the twenty-first century. Each is relevant to current events, and each has roots in the Chinese history we've presented in chapters 1, 2, and 3. Understanding these concepts and topics has helped us (and will help you, too) make sense of what China's leaders do (whether we like their actions or not).

The Pace of Change (Biànhuà de jiǎobù 变化的脚步)

Hundreds of millions of Chinese have been lifted from poverty over the last three decades of "economic reform and opening to the outside world" that began in 1978. The Chinese people, who have suffered from famine throughout their history, are living better than they ever have. This rapid modernization has meant the migration of 228 million farmers to cities (between 1978 and 2007) and the breakdown of the *hùkǒu* 户口 (permanent residence registration system), which had limited people's relocation to urban areas in the name of creating a stable and orderly environment for economic

Thought Experiment

China describes itself, and is described by others, as a developing country. But China currently has some of the most highly developed cities, a functional space program, and the second largest military in the world. On the other hand, about 15 percent of the nation lives on less than $1.25 a day (about $456 a year). What makes it advantageous for China to retain its "developing country" status, and how might that status affect the global community?

development. China has seen an explosion of youth culture and consumerism, an expansion of educational opportunity, a changing family structure, and a growing awareness of environmental issues.

Consumerism and the Disparity of Wealth (Xiāofèi zhìshàng yǔ pínfù bù jūn 消费至上与贫富不均)

In Máo's China (1949–1976), consumerism, connected with the "decadent bourgeoisie," was highly discouraged. Almost everything—from candles, matches, and clothing, to meat, eggs, and sugar—was rationed. In 1978, Dèng Xiǎopíng began to depoliticize daily life and launched economic reforms that led to growth rates equal to Japan's earlier record levels.

In the twenty-first century the Chinese state stakes its political legitimacy on a booming economy and encourages its citizens to buy goods and services previously unavailable or unaffordable. China has become the world's largest consumer of products, from cosmetics to mobile phones. By manufacturing and selling nearly 10 million cars by late 2009, China has become world's largest producer of (and market for) automobiles. The lives of tens and even hundreds of millions of consumers in urban China increasingly resemble their American, Japanese, and European counterparts.

While the consumption of name-brand items and mass-produced goods is a recent phenomenon in China, Chinese elites have historically used luxury goods as a way to create identity and communicate status. The avid consumerism of Chinese tourists awes shoppers in France, Hong Kong, and Taiwan. Young Chinese love fashion and famous world brands the same way their Western counterparts do. Being born after the Cultural Revolution (1966–1976), they could never imagine having to don the plain

Deng Xiaoping (邓小平)

Richard Nixon was known for his returns from political oblivion. Deng Xiaoping (1904–1997), head of the Chinese Communist Party (CCP) during several decades, also made several comebacks to rise to the top—a difficult thing to do in a Communist system of the last century, where the price of losing a power struggle usually meant exile, brutal imprisonment, or death.

Deng was the eldest son of a prosperous landlord. Like many of his contemporaries, he went to France through a work-study program. He then went to Moscow, where he trained as a political activist and organizer. After working briefly as a Communist Party organizer in southwest China, Deng moved to the Jiangxi Soviet to be with party leader Mao Zedong. From 1938 to 1952, Deng served in what would become the People's Liberation Army, and he led forces against the Japanese and later against Nationalist forces during the Chinese Civil War (1945–1949).

Following the civil war, the CCP rewarded Deng's loyalty by naming him vice premier in the new People's Republic. He primarily worked in the ministry of finance, creating economic policy. He later was appointed to the Politburo, and eventually became the party's general secretary. In 1966, Deng was denounced for his opposition to Mao's Socialist Education Movement (1962–1965) and removed from his post. In 1973 he was rehabilitated and returned to office, but in 1975

he was again denounced and removed from office, this time by the Gang of Four, the extremist leaders that instigated much of the Cultural Revolution (1966–1976). Following Mao's death in 1976 and the arrest of the Gang of Four, Deng again assumed a role of leadership within the Communist Party.

Through the late 1970s, Deng gradually rose to become the most influential leader in China. To modernize China's economy, he pushed for less government control, and a willingness to incorporate the best ideas and practices of other systems. His frequently quoted comment on the value of flexibility was, "It does not matter whether a cat is black or white so long as it catches mice."

Deng's embrace of flexibility and openness only went so far in the area of political freedom. He supported strong action against the Tiananmen Square protesters in 1989, a role for which he was internationally condemned. After 1989, Deng no longer held top party and government posts, but he remained an influential figure until his death in 1997. He made his final major political contribution in 1992, during a period of economic sluggishness, when at age eighty-eight he embarked on the Southern Tour. This series of impromptu visits to some of the key Special Economic Zones he had established in the early 1980s confirmed China's commitment to economic liberalization and the implementation of radical free market methods.

Thought Experiment

China currently pegs its currency to the U.S. dollar, at a rate many say is too low. Is China being a responsible stakeholder if it continues to do so? Is the height of responsibility to the Chinese people—to keep the yuan stable even if it hurts the U.S. and the rest of the world? And does it? There are those who argue that a floating exchange rate would have a minimal impact on the U.S. debt. Is the U.S. deficit a function of the its own internal policies, or a function of measures that China takes?

Mao suits in shades of green, blue, and grey that all Chinese wore during the Cultural Revolution.

The Chinese, especially those in rural areas, traditionally like to save and hate to be in debt. Escalating medical, education, and retirement costs make people in China concerned about having enough savings, and the government has begun to implement policies to alleviate those fears. Chinese and world leaders pin their hopes for domestic and global economic growth on Chinese consumer spending; the global financial and economic crisis has made Chinese leaders realize that China must boost domestic consumption instead of relying on exports.

China's economy has had double-digit growth since the late 1990s. This miraculous increase, however, hasn't spread wealth equally throughout China. The comparatively sluggish economic growth in western China could easily disrupt the nation's rapid development as a whole, while environmental degradation, ethnic minority issues, and the allocation of natural and human resources only complicates matters. According to a 2009 poll taken by *People's Forum* magazine listing the top ten concerns for the coming decade, 80.6 percent of Chinese people worry about the increasing gap between the rich and the poor. That said, a poll conducted by Pew Research Group found that the majority of Chinese are very optimistic about the future and about the direction of their country.

Some wonder, however, whether the rise of Chinese consumerism, with its reliance on a rapidly escalating use of nonrenewable resources, has created urgent questions about the sustainability of modern consumerism, in China and elsewhere. The scale and scope of environmental problems directly related to the production of consumer goods—most importantly, carbon dioxide and toxic waste—can hardly be overstated, for China and for the world.

Higher Education (Gāoděng jiàoyù 高等教育)

As China's economy has liberalized and grown, so has enrollment in China's institutions of higher education. In 1990, only 3.4 percent of young adults between the ages of 18 and 22 benefited from any form of higher education. This percentage reached 7.2 percent in 1995, 12.5 percent in 2000, 15 percent in 2002, and 23 percent in 2007, and climbed to roughly 27 million students in 2008, making China's higher education system the world's largest. In 2002, China reached the internationally acknowledged threshold of mass higher education, 15 percent of the age cohort. The increased access to higher education in all subjects is an essential component to developing the skilled workers needed to contribute to China's global ambitions. In fact, China is unique in educational history in simultaneously pushing for rapid enrollment growth, instituting new governance structures, and seeking to build world-class universities. Once funded and controlled solely by the state, today's universities must raise an increasing proportion of their operating funds from such sources as tuition fees, research grants, endowment gifts, and income from university-run enterprises. The government's embrace of a market economy has fostered the awareness that universities may be better able to contribute to economic and social development when given a considerable degree of freedom to shape their own identities and choices.

Despite the remaining government constraints on academic freedom, China's universities have become global actors, capable of holding their own in international circles of research and scholarship—in many fields of the natural sciences as well as in

Thought Experiment

Chinese students can only get into a good school if they get good test scores; essays, extracurricular activities, and interviews don't count. When they take the test, they can only apply to three schools. Do you think the focus on testing is a reliable indicator of student success? What do you think is more stressful, taking one test or completing the multifaceted and ever more elaborate college-application process so prevalent in U.S. colleges and universities? What made the focus on "tests" so ingrained in Chinese culture?

some social and professional areas of knowledge. They already have well-established patterns for offering support to countries in Africa through the training of students and through bilateral projects, and they have recently begun a series of dialogues with leading scientists and intellectuals in India to share ideas and perspectives on Asian responsibility for global development. It remains to be seen when they will be accepted as genuinely equal partners with universities in Europe and North America.

Although China's economy didn't seem to suffer as much as others from the global recession that began in late 2007, graduates still face challenges in the job market. Of the five million students who graduated from universities in 2007, 1.44 million of them were still unemployed six months after graduation. The Chinese government, anxious that large numbers of restless students might become disaffected—and mindful that student unrest was the cause of the Tiananmen protests in 1989—has initiated a plan that will help graduates find jobs in provincial and lower-level governments. In June 2009, for instance, Beijing announced a plan to hire 1,600 graduates, on three-year contracts, as assistants to officials in villages around the city.

China's Inner Life (Zhōngguó de jīngshén cengmian 中国的精神层面)

Chinese people today are acutely aware that the huge landmass they occupy has supported the longest continuous civilization in history. China's territory, often ruled by dynasties of different ethnic and geographic origins, expanded, contracted, and expanded again over the years: the problems of governing such an immense empire (and occasionally being subjected to foreign rule), made the Chinese inward looking, able to absorb ideas and influences, and less prone to designs of imperialistic expansion.

China is a country of aspiration, filled with people who want to improve their lives materially and make their country once again prominent and powerful in global affairs. Some 250 years ago, China was responsible for a large percentage of the world's production. Over time, as the Industrial Revolution progressed in Europe, China's share and role in the world economy shrank. China's economic resurgence has allowed its citizens to feel as if the country is reclaiming its honor and stepping back into its rightful place—where it stood before the United States even existed—like a family returning to its ancestral home. (See the description of the concept lǎojiā 老家 below.)

The Western "concessions" established at the end of the Opium Wars in the mid-nineteenth century left an indelible imprint on China's psyche. When Chinese talk about a century of humiliation at the hands of Western powers, they think of foreigners taking over sections of their cities, living in their country but not following their laws, establishing their own judicial systems, and making China pay—and pay. (Americans, it is important to note, did not set up concessions, but the Chinese still tend to identify the United States with the "Western powers" that treated China in this way.) This loss of dignity is reflected in the way history is told and taught to Chinese students, and it still has an enormous impact on the way twenty-first-century China approaches its relations with the West. Throwing out the Westerners after the Boxer Rebellion in 1900 and defeating the Western-supported Nationalists in 1949 were both momentous events, and China is letting the West back in on China's terms only.

China was at war (civil war, war against Japan, as an Allied power in World War II, and civil war again) for decades, from the Republican Revolution in 1911 until 1949. Warlords ruled the country in the midst of chaos during the early years of the republic; the early years of Communist rule, fraught with violence and turbulence, culminated

Eugenics Cause Happiness—a propaganda poster from 1987, nearly a decade after the inception of China's one-child policy—reinforces the program geared mainly to Han Chinese in urban areas. IISH STEFAN R. LANDSBERGER COLLECTION.

in extreme social disorder of the Cultural Revolution (1966–1976). China's current desire for stability and social harmony is not surprising, given this history.

Policies aimed at stability, however, have often resulted in stress and tensions among the populace. The one-child law, a social policy instituted in 1979 to slow China's birth rate, will continue to have major ramifications throughout the country, even though the policy has been enforced primarily in urban areas and among Han Chinese. (The government's decision to allow peasant couples to have more than one child if the first one was female was based on the recognition of reality and traditional values in the countryside—if a family didn't have a son, it wouldn't have a means of support when the parents grew old.) Family and social structures have been altered as a result. Rarely do people under age thirty-five have a sibling, which means their progeny will have no cousins, aunts, or uncles. Chinese couples have had to face complex, moral decisions about abortion—for instance, what it means to end a pregnancy to comply with the law. Chinese of all ages worry about increasingly elderly populations with no one to care for them, and only children often feel the brunt of bearing full responsibility for elderly parental and grandparental care.

Concepts: Uniquely Chinese (Zhōngguórén dúyòu de guānniàn 中国人独有的观念)

Understanding some of the concepts, philosophies, and traditions that developed over China's long cultural history help put into perspective how Chinese in the twenty-first century interact with the world.

Harmony (Hé 和)

The concept of *harmony* (*hé* 和 or *héxié* 和谐) has been an integral part of Chinese philosophical thinking for two and a half millennia. Expressed sometimes in the language of social relationships and at other times in the grander ideal of finding order in nature, it has been at the heart of various forms of Confucianism and Daoism that have appeared, disappeared, and then reappeared since the Han dynasty (206 BCE–220 CE). On the one hand, harmony was seen as most fully expressed in the classical Confucian concept of "a king acting like a king and a subject like a subject; a father like a father and a son like a son" (*jūn jūn, chén chén; fù fù, zǐ zǐ*, 君君臣臣, 父父子子). Social order was based on individuals who clearly knew their positions and understood their obligations to those above and below them. On the other hand, harmony was also seen as professed by the famed Daoist Zhuang Zi (369–286 BCE): the "oneness of nature and humans" (*tiān-rén-hé-yī*, 天人合一).

From 1989 until 2002, China promoted a system in which inequality ran rife; there were increasing disparities between the coastal regions of China and the massive inward regions, and corruption had come back stronger than ever. The liberalization of the economy had loosened many restraints on greed, personal gain, and exploitation. According to the Gini coefficient, an internationally recognized measure of social inequality, China had become one of the world's most unequal societies by 2004. The call for a "harmonious society" (*héxié shèhuì*, 和谐社会) starting in 2003 by the Chinese government under President Hú Jǐntāo 胡锦涛 and Premier Wēn Jiābǎo 温家宝, seeks to counteract social stresses caused by economic and other policies.

China's concept of "harmony" in 2010, therefore, has both sociopolitical and eco-economic dimensions. It aims to build a society in which rich and poor people, and people and nature can co-exist peacefully. China claims that its strategy for sustainable development, for instance, gives priority to people's needs and interests (*yǐ-rén-wéi-běn* 以人为本); the strategy outlines China's plan to coordinate efforts to develop the country by balancing growth between urban and rural regions, and to improve the quality of life by fostering harmony between humans and nature. This thinking, known as the "scientific outlook on development" (*kēxué fāzhǎn guān*, 科学发展观), has been written into the Constitution of the Chinese Communist Party.

Lǎojiā (老家)

The word *laojia* literally means "old home," but a more accurate translation in English is "ancestral home"—the place where one's family comes from, where one's ancestors are buried, and where one goes to worship them and expects to or hopes to be buried oneself. It is usual for new Chinese acquaintances to ask each other where their *laojia* is, and it is disconcerting to them that many modern, urbanized Westerners do not have an equivalent sense of home or place. The closest equivalent in the United States is "hometown." Even with all the turmoil of the past decades, modern Chinese still maintain the idea of *laojia*, and during extended holidays they return to visit their families. With rapid urbanization and one-child families, this concept is likely to see some transformation to fit with twenty-first-century realities.

Face (*Liǎnmiàn* 脸面)

The concept of face is not unique to China. The expressions "save face" or "lose face," terms borrowed from the Chinese *bǎo zhù miànzi* 保住面子 and *diūliǎn* 丢脸, are familiar English-language idioms. Westerners relate to the concept of "honor," which historically has led to duels and bloody feuds. "Face" is not unlike the concept of "respect" for many young, urban Westerners who interpret being "dissed" (disrespected) as a serious affront. For the Chinese, however—who use expressions like "tear up face" (*sī pò liǎn* 撕破脸), "don't want face" (*bù yào liǎn* 不要脸), "lend face" (*gěi miànzi* 给面子), and "look at my face" (*kàn wǒ miànzi* 看我面子)—the concept is perhaps more important and certainly more complex.

Topics for Further Study

Filial Piety

Governance System, Dual

Proverbs and Sayings

Tea and Tea Culture

"Face" in these contexts refers to a definition devised by the famed Chinese writer Lín Yǔtáng 林语堂: this kind of face cannot be washed or shaved, but it can be granted, lost, fought for, and presented as a gift. "Face" embodies Chinese social psychology; although abstract and intangible, it is the most delicate standard regulating Chinese social intercourse.

According to the Chinese anthropologist Hú Xiānjìn 胡先缙, two different characters for the English term "face," *liǎn* 脸 and *miàn* 面 (or *miànzi* 面子), are related but have different shades of meaning. The *liǎn* face is the respect given to one with high moral standards, while the *miàn* face is the social status or reputation gained from one's success or nurturing. In plain English, both aspects of face involve the value of someone in the eyes of others. Some scholars call *liǎn* the "moral face" and *miàn* the "social face."

When Westerners apologize using the words, "I'm sorry," it is generally assumed to mean an admission of guilt. The equivalent of this apology in Chinese is *Duì bù qǐ* 对不起, which literally means, "I'm not up to (your expectation)." The Chinese care about how others see them and how they are judged according to social norms based on the Confucian moral standards of benevolence, righteousness, propriety, trust, and knowledge. If a person fails to live up to those standards in public, he or she loses face; someone who doesn't want to see that person embarrassed must come up to "save his or her face" and justify the reasons for the mistakes or errors in order to diminish them. (In the United States, people can save face for themselves simply by using humor. Former president George W. Bush frequently made fun of himself when he mispronounced words or forgot the name of a prominent world leader.)

In China, people who blatantly disregard how others view what they do or say publicly are thought to be shameless, or, as the Chinese say it, they "don't want face." To maintain good relationships with one another, people often have to hide their negative feelings and show a good face. If they reveal their true feelings and then damage the relationship to a degree that it can't be repaired, they have "torn up their faces." This thinking supports the Chinese principle *dòu ér bù pò* 斗而不破 (fight back while still maintaining the relationship) when dealing with Western pressures. But with face (mutual respect) intact on both sides, there's always room to negotiate and to restore a damaged relationship.

The above examples explain the moral aspect of face; the following sayings deal with the social side. When Chinese people want to have something done, but they don't think they have enough clout or resources to make it happen, they will go to someone with reputation and status for help or, in the Chinese term, to "borrow his face" (*mianzi*). If the one with the *mianzi* is willing to help, he will "lend his face." Let's say a Chinese man knows that he has a good reputation in his neighborhood and is therefore respected by his neighbors. One day, his son does some damage to a neighbor's property. He will say to that neighbor, "Please look at my face (*kàn wǒ de miànzi* 看我的面子), and let him go." That means, "Please pardon my son for the sake of what you think of me, or for what I am worth in your eyes."

The Chinese look at their lives as a gift given to them by their parents. A child is therefore called "bone and flesh (*gǔròu* 骨肉)" of his parents, and siblings are called "hands and feet" (*shǒuzú* 手足). Unlike Westerners who assert their independence and individualism as they come of age, the Chinese see themselves as an extension of the family no matter when and where they are. Therefore, when Chinese youths studying in the United States achieve success, they "earn face" (zhèng liǎn 挣脸) for their families. The Chinese social face works only in a public environment, and it is so deeply rooted in the social fabric that sometimes it can't function without *guanxi* (see below).

Guānxi (关系)

Any book or magazine article about "how to do business in China" today will tell the reader that the most important thing to understand is *guanxi*, a word that means relationship. In its common usage it seems very much like Western networking, and in practice it works much like the "old boys' network." *Guanxi* is based on common experiences or connections—being a classmate or a co-worker, coming from the same area, having mutual friends. As a tool for contact and communication, *guanxi* is important in everyday Chinese life, both for individuals and groups. (*Guanxi* can also be used to imply corruption—a bit like describing someone as "connected" if they have ties to the Mafia.)

Guanxi depends largely on the Chinese view of society as a hierarchically structured order covered by an interlaced network of relationships. To make use of *guanxi*, both sides have to be able to give each other something (such as influence, protection, access to scarce goods and services, or opportunities for promotion or profit). If a person has no connection to the influential person whose *guanxi* he or she needs, a link must be created by someone from the same *guanxi* network who can, through various channels, set up the connection. For example: A requires something from D, but there is no *guanxi* between them. In A's relationship network, there is B, who is connected with C. And C has *guanxi* with D. A therefore asks B to get in touch with C. B helps A and turns to C; C wants to help B and speaks with D. D wants to do C a favor and therefore helps A. Through this sort of chain, new *guanxi* connections develop and with them new mutual obligations. In this way, *guanxi* fulfills the function of a social investment. It can be seen as a relationship among people or institutions based on exchange, and with the mutual understanding of the rights and obligations of all parties.

Qǐngkè (请客)

The opening passage of the *Analects* reflects the Confucian attitude toward entertaining friends and guests: "Is it not delightful to have friends come from afar?" Thus the proper treatment of guests has been an important duty and source of cultural pride in China for many centuries. A special term, *qǐngkè* ("to please or invite guests") continues to be used to define the processes involved in a highly developed and ritualized social art form that will be experienced by anyone who goes to China.

Qingke refers both to a straightforward goal to maintain *guanxi* (interpersonal relationships) and, more generally, to social occasions that involve entertaining friends and guests. Even as China becomes more integrated into the international community, and social relationships become more complex, acknowledging hierarchy, knowing one's place in society, reciprocating, exchanging feelings, and maintaining social harmony are behaviors still valued and maintained through the Chinese system of etiquette—from sending the invitation and orchestrating an event to saying farewell.

In China, eating and drinking are intrinsic elements of most social occasions, all of which tend to proceed according to a similar four-step pattern: *yíngkè* 迎客 (welcoming guests); *jìngchá* 敬茶 (offering guests tea, alcohol, or cigarettes); *yànqǐng* 宴请 (treating guests to a meal); *sòngkè* 送客 (seeing guests off). Hosts, of course, shoulder the burden of pleasing their guests, but guests have their own responsibilities. The practice of *zuòkè* 做客 (serving as guest) involves showering hosts with repeated compliments on the quality of the party site, the interesting group of guests, the host's thoughtfulness and attention to detail, and the amount, taste, and quality of the food and drink. Guests are further expected to remain humble, to avoid eating or drinking to excess, to avoid imposing upon the host or infringing upon the host's time in the spotlight, and to give the host every opportunity to make a good impression (save face) while participating in the occasion.

Western participants in *qingke* need to adapt to certain protocols for eating and drinking as a group, and those differ from acceptable customs while eating alone. Dishes are served family-style, and it is impolite to eat or drink if other participants present haven't started yet or have finished with the meal. Chinese events tend to be highly structured; guests only eat when the host indicates, by word or gestures, that it is time. The controlled nature of such events, combined with a host's incessant urging to eat and drink to one's fill, leads to impressions among Western participants that the focal activity of *qingke* is drinking and, in particular, getting guests drunk. In fact, the urging is not meant to be coercive—it is rather the host's attempt to fulfill the responsibility associated with *qingke,* and drinking is merely one mode of interaction involved. The primary goal of the host is to create a mirthful atmosphere that facilitates the exchange of feelings among participants.

Insider / Outsider (Nèi 内 / Wài 外)

Distinguishing between the concepts of *nèi* 内 (insider) and *wài* 外 (outsider) is critical to understanding the Chinese in terms of their interpersonal relationships and, by extension, their relationships to other cultures. The terms have long been part of the Chinese mindset, going back to the *Spring and Autumn Annals* (*Chunqiu* 春秋), one in a series of works often attributed to Confucius, that was intended to explain and expand the meaning of that great philosopher's work. In the *Annals, nei* and *wai* were used to describe how one state (an "insider") considers another state with the same ancestors to be an "outsider." But when the original "insider" state compares its relationship to a state with a different ethnic background (an even higher degree of "outsider"), the states with common ancestors consider themselves both to be "insiders."

These terms help explain how people in China make distinctions about their personal obligations: while Chinese will go to great lengths to help someone considered their own (*zìjǐrén* 自己人), meaning their family and friends, a stranger (*wàirén* 外人) in the same position could easily be ignored. This phenomenon also has implications for global relationships.

"Insiders" can be considered in terms of blood and non-blood relationships—blood relationships being those in the immediate family unit (such as parents, siblings, spouses, and children), while relatives, good friends, and intimate colleagues and classmates comprise non-blood relationships. Strangers, of course, are "outsiders," as are neighbors, colleagues, and classmates known only casually. Relationships with insiders signify trust, intimacy, closeness, mutuality, and reliability, while relationships with outsiders are characterized as difficult, courteous, and business-like. The Chinese exercise caution with outsiders, engaging only in casual conversations and seldom sharing real thoughts and private matters. Except for a courteous smile, the Chinese reveal little or no emotional feelings to outsiders. Treating insiders and outsiders differently is of practical significance to people in China: it helps to avoid hurt feelings, it promotes harmony and group solidarity, and it provides a way to manage various relationships.

As the ancient *Annals* explained, the boundary between insiders and outsiders can be mutually penetrable in different times and under different circumstances. Understanding this aspect of Chinese culture can be especially valuable in making sense of China's internal and international politics; the relationship between the Chinese Communist and Nationalist parties provides a modern example. After their initial period of cooperation (the "united front") ended in 1927, the two became enemies and were entangled in a bloody civil war until the Japanese launched its overall invasion of China a decade later. Threatened by a common outsider, the parties launched a second united front. But when the Japanese were out of the picture at the end of World War II, the Communist and Nationalists reverted to their adversarial positions and, with the establishment of the People's Republic of China in 1949, the Nationalists fled to Taiwan. In the late 1990s, faced with the rising popularity of Taiwan's pro-independence Democratic Progressive Party (DDP), the Nationalists (who saw the DDP as a political rival), and the Communists (who saw it as a threat to China's efforts to reunite with the island), came together again as insiders on the common ground of a "one China" consensus, although each claims sovereignty. This *nèi / wài* or *zìjǐrén / wàirén* complex between China and Taiwan continues to affect their future in a much broader context—one that involves the United States (which sells military defense systems to Taiwan), and Japan, with which, at the beginning of 2010, mainland China still faces disputes involving Japanese aggression prior to 1945 and territories in the East China Sea.

Challenges

Despite economic successes and promising political reforms, China today faces unique challenges as it struggles to maintain its identity and act effectively in the global community. "Balancing act" is an apt, although understated, description of the feat China must perform. No other powerful country has yet pulled it off: not the major imperial powers of the past, not the Soviet Union, and not the United States, which has its own difficulties juggling domestic and international demands.

Fulfilling responsibilities to the Chinese people, China's leaders must find solutions that work across the board: for city dwellers of the eastern seaboard and impoverished multitudes of the mountainous inland areas; for Han Chinese and China's fifty-five ethnic minorities, whose cultures and priorities clash as much as they co-exist. Tensions exist between individuals and the state—over the free exchange of information on the Internet and the government's desire to maintain China's internal political structure and top-down control of the media.

China's leaders must respond to international demands and challenges, too. As the nation increasingly takes its place on the world stage, other players up the ante and expect China to act more and more like a leader, whether by addressing climate change, acknowledging debates over human rights and the rule of law, or (like most developed countries) participating in economic globalization without allowing citizens to suffer its downsides. China is also charged with bringing together the entire global Chinese community—overseas Chinese people form significant minority groups in all parts of the world, but especially in other Asian countries and the United States.

While many policy makers and ordinary working people see China's growing position as a threat—sometimes with justification—our aim has been to show today's debates in the context of thousands of years of history and a rich cultural and philosophical tradition. *This Is China* intends to show the complexities of China and to explain why the nation is so central to our common future; we put this book in the hands of teachers and students in a spirit of hope. When the Olympic Games went to China, a full century after the Chinese first began to think about the possibility of being their host, the Chinese Olympic Committee decided upon three themes for the Games, each of which would reflect traditional Chinese thinking and values; it then came up with ways to apply them to the world's greatest celebration of global community and friendly competition. As China's role in the world grows, we can hope that the nation also aims to lend its hand to creating a future that is, as the Games were intended to be, technological, humanistic, and green.

Resources

We've compiled three lists—of books, films, and organizations—for readers who are interested in expanding their knowledge of China. As you explore the many China-related resources available today, please send additional suggestions for future printings of *This Is China* to china.updates@berkshirepublishing.com.

Further Reading

This list mixes classics and a few less-well-known titles recommended by Berkshire's editors, who chose them for their usefulness to teachers, students, and general readers alike. The fact that most of these books are written by (mostly male) Western experts, not by Chinese writers, reflects current availability, but the range of books about China, and from China, is expanding rapidly, with new contributions from Chinese and Western scholars, journalists, and novelists. Visit our website for a bibliography drawn from the 800 articles in the *Berkshire Encyclopedia of China*, and for updated versions of the lists below.

History

Barber, Elizabeth Wayland. (1999). *The Mummies of Urumchi.* New York: W. W. Norton & Company.
de Bary, Wm. Theodore et al. (Eds.). (2000). *Sources of Chinese Tradition* (2nd ed.). Volume 1. New York: Columbia University Press.
Ebrey, Patricia Buckley & Kwang-Ching Liu. (1999). *The Cambridge Illustrated History of China.* Cambridge: Cambridge University Press.
Ebrey, Patricia Buckley. (1993). *Chinese Civilization: A Sourcebook* (2nd ed.). New York: Free Press.
Fairbank, John King, & Goldman, Merle. (1998). *China: A New History.* (Enlarged ed.). Cambridge, MA: Belknap Press of Harvard University Press.
Fan Hong et al. (Eds.). (2008). *China Gold.* Great Barrington, MA: Berkshire Publishing Group.
Hessler, Peter. (2006). *Oracle Bones.* New York: HarperCollins.
Winchester, Simon. (2004). *The River at the Center of the World.* New York: Picador USA.

Modern China

Brown, Kerry. (2009). *Friends and Enemies.* London: Anthem Press.
Creek, Timothy. (2002). *Mao Zedong and China's Revolutions.* Boston: Bedford/St. Martin's.
Fenby, Jonathan. (2008). *The History of Modern China.* London: Penguin, Allen Lane.
Gifford, Rob. (2007). *China Road.* New York: Random House.
Hessler, Peter. (2001). *River Town.* New York: Harper Perennial.
Hessler, Peter. (2010). *Country Driving.* New York: HarperCollins.
Johnson, Ian. (2004). *Wild Grass.* New York: Pantheon.
Kuhn, Robert Lawrence (2010). *What China's Leaders Think.* Hoboken, NJ: Wiley, John & Sons, Inc.
Pomfret, John. (2006). *Chinese Lessons.* New York: Henry Holt and Company.
Spence, Jonathan (1999). *The Search for Modern China.* New York: W. W. Norton & Company.
Wasserstrom, Jeffrey N. (2010). *China in the 21st Century: What Everyone Needs to Know.* New York: Oxford University Press.

Biography

Kuhn, Robert Lawrence. (2005). *The Man Who Changed China: The Life and Legacy of Jiang Zemin.* New York: Crown
Spence, Jonathan. (1999). *Mao Zedong.* New York: Penguin, Viking Adult.
Winchester, Simon. (2008). *The Man Who Loved China.* New York: Harper.

127

Business and Economics

Ambler, Tim, & Witzel, Morgen. (2004). *Doing Business in China*. New York: Routledge.
Bergsten, C. Fred, et al. (2006). *China: The Balance Sheet*. New York: PublicAffairs.
Clissold, Tim. (2005). *Mr. China*. New York: Harper Paperbacks.
Hewitt, Duncan. (2007). *Getting Rich First*. London: Chatto & Windus.

Fiction

Buck, Pearl S. (2004). *The Good Earth*. New York: Simon & Schuster Adult. (Originally published 1931)
Jin, Ha. (1999). *Waiting*. New York: Pantheon.
Mones, Nicole. (2002). *A Cup of Light*. New York: Delacorte Press.
Dai Sijie. (2001). *Balzac and the Little Chinese Seamstress*. New York: Knopf.
Lu Xun. (1999). *The True Story of Ah Q*. Boston: Cheng & Tsui (originally published 1921).

Movies

Bertolucci, Bernardo. (Director). (1987). *The Last Emperor*. London: Recorded Picture Company (RPC).
Chen, Joan. (Director). (1999). *Xiu Xiu: The Sent Down Girl*. Los Angeles, CA: Image Entertainment.
Chen Kaige. (Director). (1993). *Farewell my Concubine*. Burbank, CA: Miramax.
Chen Kaige. (Director). (1984). *Yellow Earth*. China: Guangxi Film Studio.
Lee, Ang. (2000). *Crouching Tiger, Hidden Dragon*. Culver City, CA: Columbia Pictures.
Lee, Ang. (Director). (2007). *Lust, Caution*. Universal City, CA: Focus Features and River Road Productions.
Tian Zhuangzhuang. (Director). (1994). *The Blue Kite*. New York: Kino International.
Wong Kar-Wai. (Director). (2000). *In the mood for love*. Hong Kong: Block 2 Pictures.
Xie Fei/U Lan. (Director). (1986). *A Girl from Hunan*. Beijing: Beijing Film College Youth Film Studio.
Zhang Yimou. (Director). (1999). *Not one less*. Beijing: Bejing New Picture Distribution Company.
Zhang Yimou. (Director). (1992). *Raise the Red Lantern*. China: Century Communications.
Zhang Yimou. (Director). (1987). *Red Sorghum*. Xi'an, China: Xi'an Film Studio.
Zhang Yimou. (Director). (1993). *The Story of Qiu Ju*. Hong Kong: Sil-Metropole Organization.
Zhang Yimou. (Director). (1994). *To Live*. China: ERA International.
For additional suggestions see the China Movie Database: http://www.dianying.com/en/

Recommended Organizations

United States

Committee on Teaching about Asia (part of The Association for Asian Studies): http://www.aasianst.org/about/committees.htm
Asia for Educators, Columbia University: http://afe.easia.columbia.edu/
ASIANetwork: http://www.asianetwork.org/
Asia Society: Education About Asia: http://www.asiasociety.org/education-learning
China Institute: http://www.chinainstitute.org
National Committee on United States–China Relations: http://www.ncuscr.org/
National Consortium for Teaching about Asia: http://www.nctasia.org/

Europe

European Association for Chinese Studies: http://www.soas.ac.uk/eacs/home.html
Great Britain China Centre: http://www.gbcc.org.uk/
British Association for Chinese Studies: http://www.bacsuk.org.uk/
British Chinese Language Teaching Society (BCLTS): http://www.ctcfl.ox.ac.uk/clts/aboutus.htm

Australia

Chinese Language Teacher Education Centre, Melbourne Graduate School of Education: http://www.edfac.unimelb.edu.au/cttc/
Chinese Language Teachers Federation of Australia: http://www.cltfa.asn.au/frameset.htm
Chinese Studies Association of Australia: http://www.csaa.org.au/

Worldwide

Confucius Institute: http://english.hanban.org/ (This organization is hosted by many universities around the world.)

Index

BERKSHIRE ENCYCLOPEDIA OF CHINA

Modern and Historic Coverage of the World's Newest and Oldest Global Power

宝库山 中华全书: 跨越历史和现代 审视最新和最古老的全球大国

China is changing our world, and Berkshire Publishing, known for its award-winning encyclopedias on a wide array of global issues including the award-winning six-volume *Encyclopedia of Modern Asia,* is proud to publish the first major resource designed for students, teachers, businesspeople, government officials, and tourists seeking a greater understanding of China today.

"Handsome and user friendly," "charming," "generously sized illustrations," "highly recommended for academic, public, and high-school libraries."

—*Booklist* Editor's Choice

5 VOLUMES
978-0-9770159-4-8
Price: US$675
2,754 pages • 8½ × 11 inches

"Abundant photos, vignette drawings, proverbs, headings and parts of entries in pinyin and Chinese characters, and attractive layout," "the achievement of this ambitious work is admirable."

—*School Library Journal*

BERKSHIRE ENCYCLOPEDIA OF WORLD HISTORY *2ND EDITION*

Editors: **William H. McNeill,** *University of Chicago,* **Jerry Bentley,** University of Hawaii, Manoa, **David Christian,** Macquarie University, **Ralph Croizier,** University of Victoria, **John McNeill,** Georgetown University

AWARDS FOR THE 1ST EDITION	*Library Journal* Best Reference Source *Booklist* Editor's Choice *Choice* Outstanding Academic Title

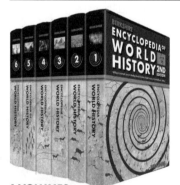

This landmark work has grown from 5 to 6 volumes and includes over 100 new articles on environmental history, world art, global communications, and information technology, as well as updates on recent events such as the Sichuan earthquake of 2008 and the global economic crisis. Hundreds of new illustrations enhance visual appeal, while updated Further Reading sections guide readers toward continued study.

"A masterful title that weaves together social, scientific, anthropological, and geographical influences on world history, this set will be the benchmark against which future history encyclopedias are compared...[it] belongs on the shelves of all high-school, public, and academic libraries. In short: buy it. Now."

—*Booklist* starred review of the first edition

6 VOLUMES
978-1-933782-65-2
Price: US$750
3,200 pages • 8½ × 11"